THE SEA ROAD

The
Sea Road

A Viking Voyage through Scotland

Olwyn Owen

Series editor: Gordon Barclay

CANONGATE BOOKS
with
HISTORIC SCOTLAND

The artist of a twelfth-century manuscript depicts a Viking fleet venturing forth.
THE PIERPOINT MORGAN LIBRARY, NEW YORK, USA

For my mother and father with love

THE MAKING
OF SCOTLAND

Series editor:
Gordon Barclay

Other titles available:

First published in Great Britain in 1999 by Canongate Books Ltd,
14 High Street, Edinburgh EH1 1TE

British Library Cataloguing in Publication Data
A catalogue record for this book is available on request from the
British Library

ISBN 0 86241 873 9

Series Design:
James Hutcheson, Canongate Books

Design:
Paul Keir

Printed in Spain by
Mateu Cromo, Madrid

Contents

Lewis Chessman
One of the Lewis chessmen, probably made in Trondheim, northern Norway. The rook was portrayed as a marauding Viking, harking back to earlier times.
NATIONAL MUSEUMS OF SCOTLAND

Prologue

There was no such place as Scotland at the dawn of the Viking Age around AD 800 – only a territory of varied geography that eventually became the Scotland of history, inhabited by different peoples, each with their own culture and customs. There was not one king, but many kings and chieftains. There were no borders; the modern boundaries of Scotland would have been meaningless to its ninth-century inhabitants. And to the sea-faring Vikings from Scandinavia, whatever contemporary territorial boundaries there were in Scotland would have been completely irrelevant. Against this background, one of the main aims of this book is to bring alive the *context* in which the Vikings operated in Scotland, and to show what part Scotland played in the Viking world.

For the Viking world was huge. From just before 800, for over 300 years, Scandinavian peoples from the modern countries of Norway, Denmark and Sweden took to the sea road in great numbers. They travelled further than Europeans had ever gone before and established a sophisticated network of communications over great distances. They exploited the riches of the East and explored the uncharted waters of the North Atlantic. They settled as farmers in the barren western lands of Greenland and discovered America 500 years before Columbus. They took part in the development of successful commercial centres from York to Kiev, and served as mercenaries at the court of Byzantium. They ravaged Christian Anglo-Saxon kingdoms; penetrated to the very heart of continental Europe and deep into Russia; and stole, extorted and traded massive quantities of silver and gold from their victims.

To be a 'Viking' during this period was to be a Scandinavian raider or adventurer, although the name probably has its root in the word *vik*, meaning inlet. To these 'inlet people', the boat or ship was their natural ally. Through their mastery of the sea they could fish, trade and communicate with their neighbours; without it, they could not survive. In their magnificent ships, they embarked on the sea road in the late eighth and ninth centuries and burst on to the European stage as raiders, warriors, traders, colonisers and political wheelers and dealers. Their contribution in extending the frontiers of Europe, in re-shaping political structures and forming powerful states, and in stimulating commerce and encouraging the growth of towns, was immense. And in many places – including Scotland – their legacy endures today.

All of this was possible only because of the strength and vibrancy of Scandinavian civilisation and culture in the Viking Age. This, then, is the other main aim of this book: to describe the way of life and imported *culture* of Scotland's Vikings and, in so doing, to qualify the barbaric image of the Vikings in popular imagination.

So let us now board our ship and sally forth with the Vikings on a voyage of discovery and colonisation – westwards, to the British Isles, and to the country we now know as Scotland.

A Viking Cargo Ship
Reconstruction drawing of a Viking cargo ship arriving in Orkney.
DAVID SIMON

The Vikings are Coming!

The fury of the northmen

A furore normannorum, libera nos, domine
From the fury of the northmen, O Lord, deliver us

In AD 789, when Beaduheard, the faithful reeve of the king of Wessex, rode out to meet three strange ships newly arrived at Portland on the south coast of England, he did not live to tell the tale. 'And they slew him ...' is the terse account in the *Anglo-Saxon Chronicle* of this first British encounter with the Vikings. Worse was to come. On 8 June 793, like 'ravenous wolves', the Vikings attacked the monastery of Lindisfarne off the coast of Northumbria, slaughtering priests and nuns, destroying everything in sight, stealing church treasures, and even taking some of the monks as slaves. The distinguished English scholar, Alcuin of York, was appalled at the ferocity of the heathen visitors and the devastation they wrought: 'Never before has such a terror appeared in Britain as we have now suffered from a pagan race, and nor was it thought possible that such an inroad could be made from the sea' he wrote.

The attacks intensified once the Vikings had discovered the coast of the British Isles to be a rich seam of easy pickings. The *Annals of Ulster* tells us that in 794 there was 'a laying waste by the heathen of all the islands of Britain', and in 798 'great devastation between Ireland and Scotland'. The entry for 795 is more specific – the raiders attacked Skye, Iona and several islands around Ireland.

The chronicling of the

Iona Abbey
The wealthy monastery of Iona proved an irresistible target and was attacked in 795, 802 and again in 806, when sixty-eight were slain. A year later, the embattled rump of the community fled to Ireland.
HISTORIC SCOTLAND

horror serves to highlight the impotence of the Vikings' victims – so much so that you would think that the suddenness and ferocity of the Viking raids disturbed an otherwise Utopian age of peace and prosperity. But even a cursory reading of the *Anglo-Saxon Chronicle* reveals the extent and frequency of Anglo-Saxon violence against one another; while Ireland and Scotland remained hotbeds of internecine warfare throughout the period. Even the monastic communities were not above brutal retaliation if the opportunity arose. When a storm destroyed Viking ships attacking Jarrow in 794, the few men who reached the shore 'were immediately killed at the mouth of the river'.

There are no contemporary Scottish accounts and so we must rely on the evidence of a few English and Irish sources. These give the Vikings a uniformly hostile press. There was more to this than 'better the devil you know'. Although the sudden appearance of ferocious foreigners who looked and sounded nothing like anything previously encountered must have been alarming to say the least, one fact above all others united the Vikings' victims in horror against them – they were pagans. These were the 'ravages of heathen men' against the Christian west – and the Vikings have left no contemporary testimony to challenge the accepted view.

And so it was that their literate and learned Christian victims had the last laugh. It was their epitaph on the Vikings that lasted, that gave us the dreaded heathens, pirates and barbarians of popular imagination through the ages. Through their eyes, the Vikings became the stuff of legend, their dreadful exploits and heroic deeds of derring-do lamented and extolled in more or less equal measure through the centuries – by writers, historians, artists and film-makers.

And yet this is only a tiny part of the story of the Vikings. The Vikings might have been alien to the Christian west, but theirs was a civilisation nonetheless, with a vigorous culture and an established system of law and social stratification. The people of Scandinavia shared a common inheritance, a common language, a common art and a common religion – different from those of Christian Europe, but no less valid. So who were these men and women of the north? And why did they suddenly take to the sea road, in a great outpouring of peoples that was to have such an impact not only on Scotland and the British Isles, but also on large parts of Europe and beyond?

Exodus from the homelands

What caused an exodus from Scandinavia is one of the enduring conundrums of history, but at least part of the answer lies in geography. Scandinavia covers a vast area: if you were to leave its northern tip, well inside the Arctic Circle, and travel to Rome, you would only be halfway when you reached southern Denmark, having travelled some 1200 miles. But much of the interior of the Scandinavian landmass was unsuitable for settlement, characterised by near-impassable barriers of high mountains, dense forests and deep bogs. The long indented coastline, numerous islands and inland water-ways meant that the lives of its inhabitants were always dominated by water, their settlements and farms perched at the water's edge. Norway's western shore is cut by fjords, some extending over a hundred miles inland. From one fjord settlement to the next, it was the highway of the sea that joined people together – and joined the people of Norway to their neighbours in the settled parts of Sweden and Denmark, in a pattern of scattered farmsteads. So the sea was an obvious route to choose for

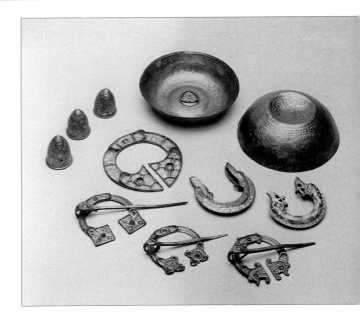

St Ninian's Isle Hoard
The great treasure of Pictish silver found on St Ninian's Isle, Shetland, is thought to have been buried in response to the Viking threat.
NATIONAL MUSEUMS OF SCOTLAND

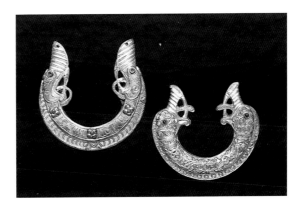

'Norman Pirates of the Ninth Century'

The Vikings have gone down in popular imagination as rapists
and pillagers. The artist of this 1894 painting, the French painter
Evariste Vital Luminais, was interested in medieval history and
the weapons shown are fairly in period; but the ship prow (in the
background) owes more to romanticism than to the then recently
discovered Gokstad Viking ship.

MUSÉE ANNE DE BEAUJEU, MOULINS, FRANCE

Scandinavians who wished to leave. But why
did the Scandinavians suddenly begin to leave
in such large numbers in the ninth century?

Duddo, a priest writing in Normandy in
about 1020, blamed over-population in the
homelands; while the writers of the thirteenth-
century Icelandic sagas thought that the
tyranny of those in power had caused mass
emigration. Both were undoubtedly factors. In
this heroic society, the demonstration of male
virility was important, and an increase in
population the inevitable result. The most
fertile and easily worked areas had been settled
since prehistoric times; in the Viking Age,
settlement spread and intensified wherever
farming was viable, helped by an improvement
in the climate and developing farming technology; ironically, these improvements stimu-
lated further population growth. In Norway,
political organisation of these scattered, inde-
pendent groups only came in the time of King
Harald Finehair, from about 890; but earlier
attempts to foist political control may well
have provoked waves of emigration.

With hindsight, this exodus from the
homelands fuelled a great Scandinavian enter-
prise. But it is important to remember that this
was not an organised exodus. The average
boatload of Vikings, whether Norwegians
setting sail for Greenland or Swedes setting out
for Baghdad, was not aware of the Viking
impact overall on the early medieval
world. The Vikings' own world
view was pragmatic and opportun-
ist, and they were driven by a range
of imperatives – adventure, plunder,
trade, colonisation. What began as
an adventure could soon develop
into an established trade route or
colony – and once news reached

View of the Aurlandsfjord, Sogn

This typically rugged landscape prompted the
Norwegians to take to the sea road. Norway's
average altitude is 500 metres above sea-level, but
its western shore is punctuated by fjords, some
extending far inland.

MAGNAR DALLAND

Lords of the seas

The Viking ship may not have caused the Viking Age, but it did make it possible – this was the Viking achievement *par excellence*. The Vikings' legendary superiority in shipbuilding technology and their supreme navigational skills allowed them to travel further, faster and more surely than their contemporaries.

The Viking tradition of shipbuilding was characterised by slender and flexible boats, with symmetrical ends and a true keel, producing longships capable of high speeds at full sail. The ships were exceptionally seaworthy, light in the water and easy to beach, which made surprising assaults and swift withdrawals possible. There were several types of Viking ship: as well as warships, there were ocean-going cargo ships, coastal traders and smaller boats for fishing and local journeys. Boats varied in length from about 6 to 30 metres, and were powered either by a combination of the famous square sail and oars, or by oars alone. The Vikings navigated mainly by memorising the coastlines and using simple astronomical observations. Only when they sailed due west would they have needed a navigational instrument; a wooden disc found in Viking Greenland was probably part of a simple sunlight/shadow compass.

By sea, Bergen lies nearer to Scotland than Stockholm. Little wonder then that when the Viking Age began, around 780, the Norwegians should turn westwards – to Scotland.

The Gokstad Ship

The magnificent Gokstad ship, buried in south-east Norway in about AD 900 and excavated in 1880, was over 23 metres long and built of oak. Its remarkable 17.6 metre long keel was carved from a single oak timber. In 1893, a replica voyaged from Norway to Newfoundland in just twenty-eight days and attained a speed of 11 knots.

UNIVERSITETETS OLDSAKSAMLING MED VIKINGSKIPSHUSET, OSLO, NORWAY

Rover Badge of a Viking Ship

The Viking ship has become something of an emblem for the age and is an immediately recognisable symbol even today – here we see it on the badge of a modern Rover car.

ROVER GROUP LTD

home of the opportunities that lay to west, east and south, more boatloads of adventurers, merchants and settlers inevitably followed.

Scotland in the Viking Age

Early historic Scotland was an amalgam of peoples – Picts, Scots, Gaels, Angles and Britons – all competing for territory against a backdrop of shifting allegiances. The very name 'Scotland' would have brought looks of blank incomprehension to our warring early historic ancestors at the beginning of the Viking Age. These were tumultuous and insecure times, with tribes and kindred repeatedly pitted against each other. The earliest 'Scots' were not Scottish in any sense that we would understand, but Dál Riata Gaels from north-east Ireland. By the early ninth century these Irish Gaels were installed in Argyll and the Inner Hebrides, from where they vied for supremacy with the Britons in Strathclyde and the south-west, the Angles in the south and south-east, and the Picts in the agricultural heartlands of the east and north. The Picts were descended from the indigenous Celtic tribes and occupied most of mainland Scotland north of the Forth–Clyde line. Only a linguistic accident gave us 'Scotland' rather than 'Pictland'.

It was into this kaleidoscope of warring factions that Scandinavians first trespassed, shortly before the year 800. Sailing west across open water from Norway, the Vikings' first landfalls would have been Shetland and Orkney, in the territory of the Picts. Within a comparatively short time – perhaps about 50 years – the Northern Isles had effectively become a Norwegian colony. It is hard to believe that this was achieved peacefully, but what happened to the Picts in these islands remains an archaeological mystery. They simply vanish from the record, perhaps absorbed into the new mainstream culture.

The Orkney earldom rapidly became the centre of Norse power in Scotland. From Orkney the Scandinavians would eventually

also control large parts of northern Scotland. By the mid eleventh century, the Norwegian earl of Orkney dominated all the maritime parts of Scotland north of the Great Glen.

From Orkney and Shetland, the Vikings could sail within sight of land all the way south-west to Ireland and the Irish Sea, via the Western Isles, south-west Scotland and the Isle of Man. These island stepping stones were the ideal Viking sailing route, an extended coastline – just like home. And, as in Orkney and Shetland, Scandinavian traders and settlers followed the raiders along this western sea road, colonising large parts of the western fringe and Argyll, and establishing important bases around the Irish Sea. Here, too, the Vikings had a major impact on the tortuous history of early Scotland. Ultimately, it was their presence and expansionist tendencies which led to the unification of the Gaels and the Picts in the later ninth century, and forced the centre of the emerging Scottish kingdom to move eastwards, to Scone, under the mac Alpin kings.

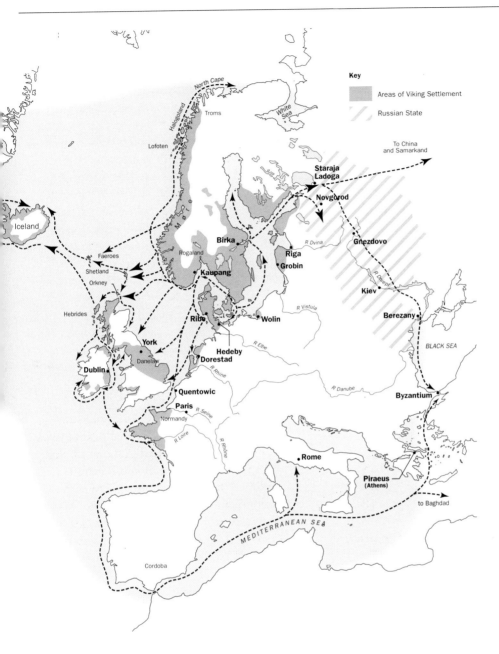

**Viking Age
Scandinavia and
the Viking World**
Showing the routes
taken by the Viking
raiders, traders and
settlers.
ROB BURNS

Key

Areas of Viking Settlement

Russian State

This new Scandinavian axis, stretching north and west around the Scottish coasts and down to Dublin, remained an important element of Scotland's political geography for centuries after the Viking Age. Only very gradually were these insular communities drawn into the Scottish medieval kingdom. Even today, the cultural roots of Orkney and Shetland lie in their Scandinavian heritage.

A NOTE ABOUT DATING AND CHRONOLOGY

The Viking Age is normally dated from around 800 to 1100, but this neat dating bracket quickly crumbles away when we look at Scotland. The Viking presence in the Northern Isles is traditionally thought to date from around AD 800 but documentary sources for Scotland in this early period are totally absent. We know

that Viking raids were having an impact around the coasts of Britain and Ireland from around 790, so it is *probable* that pirate bases, and perhaps settlements, were established in the Northern and Western Isles about then; but if we look at the 100 or so pagan Viking graves in Scotland, the earliest date from about the middle of the ninth century.

If it is hard to pinpoint the start of the Viking Age in Scotland, it is even harder to pinpoint the end. The traditional end date of the Viking Age – about 1100 – means absolutely nothing in the Scandinavian areas of northern and western Scotland. Twelfth- and thirteenth-century Orkney and Shetland, in particular, remained completely Norse in culture. Indeed, the islands remained under the control of the Norwegian Crown until 1468. Even the Western Isles remained subject to Norway until 1266. Sometimes, we describe the period from about 1100 to about 1300 in these areas as 'Late Norse'. I prefer not to try to fit 'Viking Scotland' into a dating strait-jacket, but simply to accept that Scandinavian culture became embedded in the north and west of the country in the ninth century, developed its own momentum and endured as the dominant culture there for some 500 years; and its influences still linger today.

Viking Ship at Sea
A modern replica of a Viking ship at sea
VIKINGESKIBSHALLEN I ROSKILDE, DENMARK

Viking Fleet
This fleet is carved on a piece of wood found at Bryggen (Bergen), Norway.
BRYGGENS MUSEUM, BERGEN, NORWAY

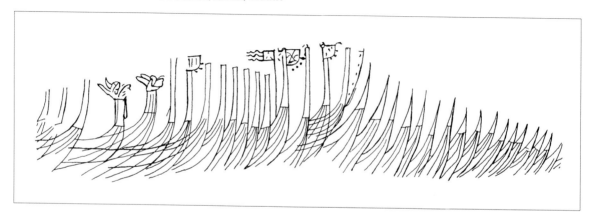

The North Way and the Orkney Earldom

The creation of the Orkney earldom

The first Vikings in Orkney and Shetland probably captured headlands and promontories to use as raiding bases. At first things must have been fairly unruly, with Vikings based in the islands attacking each other, Scotland's north and west coasts, and even marauding back in Norway during the summers. We do not know quite how this state of affairs turned into political conquest. The prelude to large-scale colonisation by Norwegian farmers must have been reasonably peaceful conditions. We think these came about when the powerful Møre family dynasty, from west Norway, established political control over the islands in the later ninth century.

Our main documentary source is the Viking sagas, especially the wonderful *Orkneyinga Saga*. But these were written over 300 years later – when their Icelandic authors felt it prudent to describe the islands' conquest in terms of the power and generosity of the then king of Norway's ancestors. The traditional story is that King Harald Finehair granted

Sties of Brough
An aerial photograph of the Sties of Brough, Sanday, Orkney, where Viking graves were probably inserted into earlier, prehistoric burial mounds. This site was recently investigated by the Time Team for Channel 4 television. The first boatloads of Viking settlers found the low-lying fertile green islands of Orkney laid out like jewels in the ocean – and theirs for the taking.
MICK ASTON

the earldom of Orkney to Rognvald of Møre, in compensation for the loss of his son. In fact, the Møre family was probably a thorn in King Harald's side at a time when he was attempting to unify western Norway; and, when Rognvald and his sons conquered the islands, it was easiest for Harald to seem to be in control of events by granting them the earldom. Rognvald promptly gave the islands to his brother, who became Sigurd the Mighty, first Earl of Orkney. Sigurd and another great Viking warrior, Thorstein the Red, then conquered, and added to the earldom, Caithness, Sutherland, Moray and Ross.

However it happened, from about the year 850, Viking dominion in the Orkney earldom went unchallenged and Norse farmers began to flood into the islands. In Orkney and Shetland we see Norse culture and civilisation at its purest in Scotland, for the Vikings transplanted their way of life and material culture almost wholesale from Norway to the Northern Isles.

When the first boatloads of Viking settlers from the rugged west coast of Norway arrived in Orkney, they must have thought they had landed in paradise. The well-drained light soils, and the mild climate of cool summers and warm winters, would have made Orkney and north-east

Caithness especially attractive; but in Shetland, too, the Norsemen found a home from home, where a maritime way of life was easy, and a living could be made from a combination of pastoral farming, fishing and fowling. Viking Age farms in Norway were as self-supporting as possible in terms of food and other basic commodities, with arable land always at a premium. In the Northern Isles, too, the first settlements were probably centred on the best arable lands, with secondary lands parcelled out to newcomers and second or third generation Norse colonisers.

Making a living in the Orkney earldom

The first thing the new settlers needed was strong, warm and wind-resistant houses, just as at home. But in Scandinavia, Viking houses were built mainly of wood; in almost treeless Orkney, Shetland and Caithness, the Vikings had to learn how to build in other materials – stone for walls; turf and earth for insulation in wall cores; larger driftwood for structural and roof-bearing timbers; peat and smaller driftwood for fuel; and heather, turf and grasses for roofing.

Good building stone was readily available in the sandstone beds that make up so much of Orkney, Caithness and parts of Shetland. In many cases the Norse took over existing farms, building on top of the abandoned Pictish buildings. But the houses they built were usually entirely different.

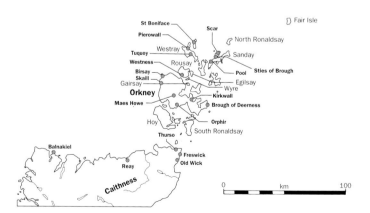

Map
Sites mentioned in the Orkney earldom.
ROB BURNS

Farming, fishing and daily life

Contrary to our image of the Vikings as pirates and warlords, most excavated Norse settlements have proved to be simple farms, even where *Orkneyinga Saga* shows their owners to have been people of standing and wealth. As at home in Scandinavia, the physical environment dictated the settlers' way of life. Their activities followed the pattern of the seasons as they exploited all the available resources.

Farming was the mainstay of the settlers – as it had been in earlier times. Animal bones and other detritus from the middens of excavated settlements show that Norse farmers mainly raised sheep and cattle, but also kept pigs, goats, ponies and hens. The small, sturdy cattle and somewhat hairy sheep seem mostly to have been slaughtered young, for their meat, hides and horns. The ponies they bred were a little bigger than modern Shelties, and were perhaps used for ploughing or bringing in the peats; sometimes they were also eaten.

Orphir Mill
One of the earliest examples anywhere of a Norse horizontal water-mill for the milling of grain was built at Orphir, Orkney. Here we see the tail-race leading from what would have been the under house of the mill. When the tail-race fell out of use, it became filled with rubbish from the Late Norse Earl's Bu (hall complex) nearby.
CHRISTOPHER MORRIS

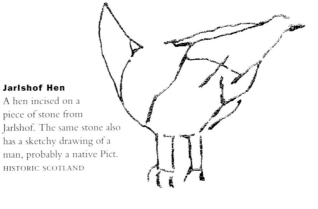

Jarlshof Hen
A hen incised on a piece of stone from Jarlshof. The same stone also has a sketchy drawing of a man, probably a native Pict.
HISTORIC SCOTLAND

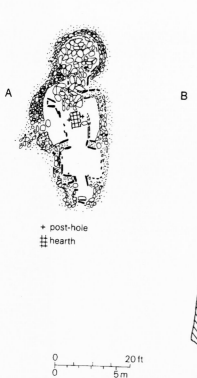

A

+ post-hole
# hearth

0 ———————— 20 ft
0 ——————— 5 m

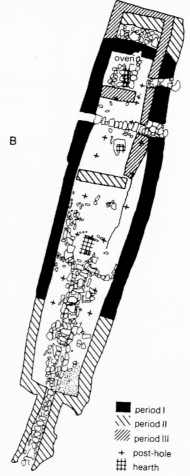

B

oven

■ period I
⧄ period II
▨ period III
+ post-hole
# hearth

House Plans

Typical Pictish and Viking
house-plans: A) Pictish
Buckquoy, Birsay, Orkney
(after Anna Ritchie); B)
Viking Jarlshof, Shetland (after
J.R.C. Hamilton).
The Vikings replaced the
cellular and circular structures
of their Pictish predecessors
with distinctive rectangular
longhouses – the precursor
of the crofting blackhouse
– and introduced an
architectural tradition to
Scotland's highlands and
islands that endured with
little modification into the
nineteenth century.

Viking houses in the Northern Isles

Jarlshof, at the southern tip of Shetland, only 48 hours by the sea road from Norway, was home to 12 or more generations of Norse settlers over some 500 years, and has become something of a type site for Viking settlement in Scotland. The first longhouse was over 21m long by 6m wide and had slightly bowed walls up to 1.5m thick. The low walls had faces of coursed stone with a central core of turf and compacted earth, and the roof was thatched, probably with heather and turf. Nearby were two or three smaller buildings, including a byre, a pen for livestock, and perhaps a smithy and bath house. The house was fairly spacious inside, organised around a long fire which ran down the centre of the building, flanked on both sides by low earthen benches against the walls. This was the typical early Norse hall-house, with kitchen, living and sleeping space all within the one long room. Any partitions would have been only light screens of wattle or planks.

Later on, more houses and yards were built at Jarlshof, but now the houses had the living quarters and byre under one roof, with stables and other outbuildings nearby. The original house was also lengthened and a byre attached to one end. What happened here was typical of Late Norse architecture after about 1100, and can be seen all over the Orkney earldom.

Recent surveys on the northern Shetland island of Unst have identified the remains of possible Norse farms at up to 30 different locations. The best preserved is at Hamar, where a classic longhouse, 23m long, with curved walls and rounded corners, lies aligned downslope. It resembles the early Norse houses on the Brough of Birsay, Orkney, which was the political centre of the Orkney earldom and is one of the best preserved settlements anywhere in the Viking world. Here, clusters of hall-houses, barns and byres lie scattered across the slope and along the cliff edge, most of them aligned downslope to help with drainage. Interestingly, the same building plots were maintained from Pictish times through more than 400 years of Norse building and re-building on the Brough.

But, overall, surprisingly few early Viking Age settlements have been found in the Orkney earldom; most date to later than about 1100. Some houses may have been built mainly of wood, imported from Norway, and other organic materials such as turf, which would make them hard to find archaeologically. Others may have been replaced by later farms on the same site, hiding all trace of the earlier structures. To complicate matters, we are beginning to realise that our models of early Viking settlement and house types are probably too simplistic. We know the Vikings often colonised earlier settlement sites; what we had not appreciated until recently was that sometimes they continued to use parts of previous structures, even where these did not conform to Viking building fashions. For instance, at Pool, a prehistoric and Viking site on Sanday, parts of some of the earlier Pictish buildings continued in use almost until the end of the Norse period of occupation.

Alan Sorrell's reconstruction of Jarlshof Viking village
HISTORIC SCOTLAND

Jarlshof
The first Viking hall-house at Jarlshof; with inset of Jarlshof from the air.
HISTORIC SCOTLAND

Cereals were grown wherever possible, mainly hulled six-row barley (bere) and oats, for making meal, porridge and oatcakes; several types of traditional Orkney and Shetland oatcake still have Norse names. But crop growing was not only about bare subsistence. The Norse also introduced the cultivation of flax, which was used for the production of linseed oil, cake and fibre; linen cloth was highly valued by the Vikings.

The Vikings varied and supplemented their diet by inshore fishing, especially for cod, saithe and ling. In Shetland, where it was difficult to grow enough cereals to provide meal all the year round, dried fish may have been used as often as bread.

THE 'FARM MOUND' PHENOMENON

On Orkney's northernmost islands – Sanday, North Ronaldsay and Papa Westray – there are great 'farm mounds', varying in diameter from 50m to over 200m, with deposits sometimes more than 4m thick, built up over several thousand years of occupation. Many of the farms on the summits of these mounds are still in use and the farm-names contain Norse elements, such as 'how' (from the Old Norse *haugr*, mound), demonstrating that the mounds already existed when the Norse arrived and were re-used by the colonisers.

Similar-looking settlement mounds occur in the far north of Norway, where they are composed mainly of turf, from the repeated building and disintegration of turf and timber houses. At first it was thought that the Orkney mounds must also consist largely of building debris and sand-blow; but trial excavations on three mounds in Sanday showed that the bulk of their immense volume is composed of stone-free deposits, notably fuel ash and turves. This material would have been excellent manure, so why wasn't it used? Perhaps Sanday was so fertile that it was not necessary for farmers to spread the ash over the fields?

Two recent excavations have shown that things may not be this clear-cut. At St Boniface, Papa Westray, the farm mound is made up of two distinct accumulations of material, separated by a long-standing soil. A 1-metre high mound of fuel ash and refuse built up slowly just before the Viking Age began. But then, in the 1100s, a further 3 metres of ash, fish processing waste and other debris accumulated in the space of only a few decades. It seems that the twelfth-century folk at St Boniface were specialist fishermen who burnt massive quantities of turves, possibly while rendering down fish livers for oil. These northern Orkney islands lack peat, and turf was evidently the alternative fuel of choice. Burn-

ing turf produces ten times as much ash as burning peat, but if the Late Norse occupants were primarily fishermen, not farmers, they had no need to spread it on the fields as fertiliser.

The eroding farm mound at Pool, Sanday, has extensive Neolithic and Iron Age deposits, including stone structures, underlying a Norse settlement. Here, as elsewhere, the Viking presence was part of a long process of cultural development, rather than a disconnected interval of colonisation. There is a clearly identifiable period of overlap between the thriving pre-Norse farming community and the Viking presence. Radiocarbon dates from the earliest, securely Viking layers indicate Norse occupation well in advance of the creation of the earldom in the later 800s; and from the very earliest phase of Viking settlement, Pool was a well-founded settlement with houses and outbuildings.

St Boniface
A detail of the eroding farm mound at St Boniface, Papa Westray, Orkney, which formed during two main episodes: a mound about one metre high built up over 200 years just before the Viking age; and then, in the space of a few decades in the twelfth century, a 3-metre depth of Norse fuel ash, fish processing waste and other refuse accumulated very rapidly.
HISTORIC SCOTLAND

A Viking Farm

A reconstruction drawing of life on a Viking farm in the
Northern Isles.

DAVID SIMON

WHY WERE THERE NO VIKING TOWNS IN THE EARLDOM?

Nowhere in the earldom have we found evidence for a typical Viking town – like the Scandinavian centres of manufacturing and trade located on major maritime routes. Even on the Brough of Birsay, Orkney, the only evidence for industry is a Late Norse smithy for the production and repair of iron tools and weapons. The Brough was the political centre of the earldom, and it was normal for the aristocracy's residences to be quite separate from commercial centres; but there is surprisingly little evidence for manufacturing or *kaupangr* (market places) anywhere in the Northern Isles.

Some locations are obvious candidates for early Viking Age beach markets. The wide, shallow bay at Pierowall, Westray, perhaps Orkney's best natural harbour, probably attracted a periodic beach market, where settlers and traders – passing through on their way to more lucrative markets – might exchange or barter goods. Perhaps this is where someone from Tuquoy, in the south of the island, acquired a fine maple handle? No Viking settlement has yet been found here, but a pagan Viking cemetery, with at least 17 graves, was discovered in the nineteenth century through sand-blowing and piecemeal excavations.

Not before the early eleventh century do we have evidence of a developing town in the Orkney earldom – as in much of the rest of medieval Scotland in a different political context. Indeed, Kirkwall, first mentioned in *Orkneyinga Saga* in 1046, has been described as *Norway's* oldest town on its original site.

Brough of Birsay

The Brough: views from the air, and from the other side of the causeway. The number of Viking longhouses scattered across the slope on the Brough of Birsay, a tidal island, shows a community larger than the usual family unit – but even here there is nothing of the typical Viking town.

HISTORIC SCOTLAND

Brough of Birsay

The Brough: excavation of a Viking house in progress; a well-preserved Viking house; and plan of settlement. Typical and not so typical Viking houses survive on the Brough of Birsay, Orkney, renowned as one of the best preserved settlements anywhere in the Viking world. Recent excavations have shown much more diversity in house types than we might have expected.

HISTORIC SCOTLAND/OLWYN OWEN

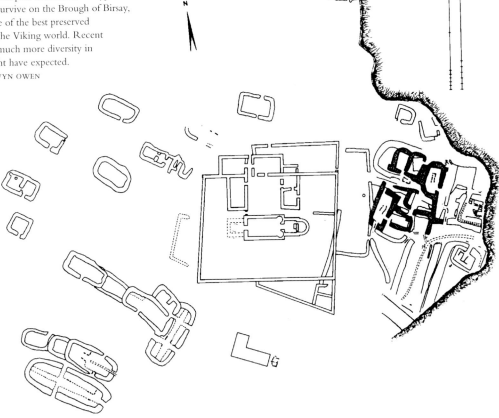

Beach Market

A reconstruction drawing of a beach market – this one at Pierowall, Westray, with its
good natural harbour – where settlers and traders might exchange or barter goods.
DAVID SIMON

One reason for the apparent lack of early Norse trading settlements in the north probably lies in the nature of society in the homeland. The Viking settlers came overwhelmingly from widely dispersed settlements along the long coastline of western Norway, where no Viking towns have so far been discovered. Kaupang, on the Oslo fjord in eastern Norway, is the only Norwegian site to qualify as a Viking market place earlier than the eleventh century. In this society of developing chiefdoms, surpluses were rendered to the chief through hospitality and feasts; the relationship was cemented by exchanging gifts, probably at agreed farms rather than fixed centres. This system, or something very like it, was probably transplanted to the Orkney earldom by the early Norse settlers.

There is plenty of evidence in the Orkney earldom for the import of craft goods and other objects from Scandinavia, especially in the objects buried in pagan graves, many brought with them by the incoming settlers. But the Northern and Western Isles lay on an important trade route between the Scandinavian homelands and the area round the Irish Sea, especially Dublin, probably the richest port in west Britain at that time. Access to goods and wealth was easy and there was little impetus to develop into a centre of trade themselves. Although passing trade and exchange must have taken place on a small scale in the Northern Isles, the settlers grew wealthy as a result of their geographical relationship with Dublin and the Irish Sea area. The best evidence for that lies in the Viking silver hoards, found in all areas of Scandinavian Scotland.

David Simon '98

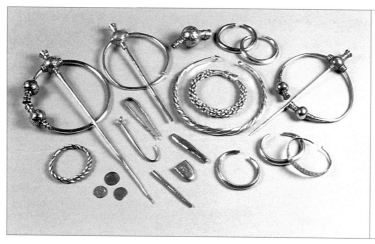

Skaill Hoard

Part of the great Skaill hoard, Orkney, which weighed over 8kg in total. The hoard was buried in a pre-existing substantial mound, and would have been easy to find again later on. This suggests that the owner probably meant to recover the hoard.

NATIONAL MUSEUMS OF SCOTLAND

Thistle brooch

Some brooches are decorated with vibrant Viking animal art, typical of the Mammen style of ornament. These brooches were a conspicuous display of wealth, worn by men on their cloaks – but only on special occasions. They would have been lethal in everyday use; the hoops were up to 17cm across and the pins 40cm long.

NATIONAL MUSEUMS OF SCOTLAND

VIKING SILVER

The economic system was based on barter and the exchange of silver – highly prized by the Vikings. Hoards of silver were buried in the ground for safekeeping, but a bizarrely high quantity was never recovered by its owners – for reasons that we do not know – leaving it to be found in modern times. Given that the hoards we know about must represent only a small proportion of the silver in circulation, the sheer quantity testifies to the accumulation of great wealth in Scandinavian Scotland, especially in the tenth and eleventh centuries.

The largest Viking treasure from Scotland was unearthed by a boy in 1858, from a rabbit burrow at Skaill, Orkney. This massive hoard, originally buried around AD 950–970, contained about 115 objects, including great neck-rings, brooches, arm-rings, pins, ingots, ring-money and hack-silver (cut-up pieces of objects). There were also 21 Arabic coins, but coins were just another form of bullion or scrap silver. Many objects and fragments were 'nicked' to test the silver quality, with the number of 'nicks' on a single item perhaps showing roughly how many times it had changed hands. The ring-money is a sort of wearable currency – plain, almost complete rings of an approximate standard weight. Ring-money as a form of currency was probably created earlier in the tenth century in the area of the Irish Sea; indeed, an Irish Sea source is likely for many objects in the Skaill hoard.

The Skaill hoard's most striking component is the huge and beautifully decorated 'thistle brooches', so called because of the 'brambled' ornament on some of their terminals. These almost certainly arrived in Orkney from somewhere in the Irish Sea area; some are so similar that they may be the work of an individual craftsman, or at least a single workshop.

This mixture of apparently 'active' silver, for use as payment, gifts or in exchange, and prestige ornaments in good condition, suggests that this was not a merchant's hoard, but more likely the accumulated capital of a Norse chieftain or a leading family within the community. Skaill was, in fact, one of Orkney's prime settlement locations. We know this from its name.

Tuquoy and the wonders of waterlogging

Bone and carbonised seeds are well preserved in the shell sands of southern Shetland, Orkney and Caithness, which is why archaeological sites in these areas frequently produce huge quantities of evidence for fishing and farming. But it is very rare for organic materials to survive – wood, leather, unburnt plants and seeds – all of which were undoubtedly important in the settlers' daily life.

This is why we in the excavation team were excited, during excavations at Tuquoy, Westray, in Orkney, to discover a large waterlogged tenth-century pit, actually on the beach. At its base was a nasty-smelling, 'sticky', black, wet fill 60cm deep. Laboratory analyses showed that it largely comprised animal dung, straw and ash. It also contained unburnt wood, peat, twigs, grasses, leather scraps, shells, insects, pollen and other microscopic remains. This type of rare discovery has the capacity to revolutionise our understanding of the environmental basis of Norse Orkney.

Norse period Orkney was not entirely treeless, with sparse patches of willow scrub and, perhaps, birch and hazel. From the pit came a carved birch handle, and willow twigs and branches fashioned into small domestic articles and used as twine, perhaps to hold down roofs. All other species of tree arrived either as driftwood or traded imports. Here, for the first time, in the sheer quantity of pine offcuts from the trimming of planks, we have evidence for the large-scale importation of wood. The trunks had been cut to squared cross-sections at source, probably in Norway, for ease of transportation. Ready-made objects were also imported: there was a fine handle of maple; small quantities of oak used for carpentry; and ash for handles, hafts and shafts. Offcuts of larch and spruce demonstrate that driftwood was used in buildings as well as for fuel. The wood assemblage also furnishes evidence for a range of tools: knives, spoon-bits, axes, adzes and, probably, a plane with a 1.8cm wide blade; while the presence of roughouts and unfinished objects also testifies to an active, domestic, wood-working industry.

The varied insect fauna included both indoor and outdoor species, insects associated with decomposing material, and human and animal parasites. Only in the insect assemblage do we see evidence for wool-processing at Tuquoy; while the insects also confirm that peat, hay and seaweed were all being brought into the buildings for a variety of purposes. The inhabitants of Tuquoy were apparently infested with lice and fleas indicating low levels of hygiene – a suspicion reinforced by the numbers of species associated with rotting organic matter. Similar conditions occurred in near contemporary deposits from Iceland, Greenland, Oslo, Dublin and York. To be fair to the Vikings, these conditions were almost certainly the norm in much of the past.

This successful Viking Age farm clearly relied on a mix of arable and pasture. The deposit was extraordinarily rich in cereal pollen, primarily oats and barley, together with arable weeds and species indicating pasture nearby. Some of the weeds and herbs were probably also used in cooking and for medicinal purposes. Interestingly, the cereals and weeds were all mixed together, perhaps through reaping the cereal stalks for straw, suggesting that bedding material for stalled animals is represented here.

So was the 'pit' actually the sunken floor of a byre? The environmental evidence is somewhat contradictory, and matters are not helped by the fact that we could only excavate part of it; but the most likely interpretation is that this is a byre floor with an intact accumulation of byre-manure, whose constituents included household refuse incorporated into the animal bedding.

The Tuquoy Pit
The waterlogged pit on the beach at Tuquoy, during excavation.
HISTORIC SCOTLAND

Birch Handle
Of three pieces of birch, one was a carved handle covered with a crude geometric pattern, and shows the Vikings' fondness for decorating domestic objects.
HISTORIC SCOTLAND

The Scar boat burial

In the winter of 1991, a Viking boat burial eroding out of the low cliff at Scar, Sanday, Orkney, was dramatically 'rescued' by archaeologists just before it was washed away by winter storms. This was a most unusual burial, not least because the 7.15m long, oak rowing boat contained, not one, but three bodies: a man aged about 30 when he died, a child of about ten, and a woman who may have been in her seventies – an extraordinarily great age by the standards of the time. The people who buried the Scar woman had almost certainly never known anyone this old (the average medieval life-span was about 35 years) and, for the last 30 years of her life, she must have been a figure of increasing awe

and reverence. What she herself made of this biological uniqueness, we can only imagine.

Some of the grave had already been lost to the sea, but it was still richly furnished with goods. The man had a sword in its scabbard, a quiver of eight arrows, 22 gaming pieces (originally in a container), a fine comb, two lead weights, and perhaps a shield. On the basis of the surviving finds, he seems to have been equipped primarily as a warrior who enjoyed some leisure time!

The woman was accompanied by a magnificent carved whalebone plaque, a gilded bronze brooch, a comb, two spindle whorls (discs used in spinning yarn), a pair of shears, a needle tidy containing two iron

needles, an iron weaving batten, a small sickle, and a maple box. The brooch and the whalebone plaque are truly exceptional finds – and suggest that this woman belonged to the upper levels of society. This impression is reinforced by the concentration of items associated with weaving and sewing: textile production was a common activity of wealthy, well-placed Viking women.

Modern scientific excavation shines a powerful light on the past. To give one tiny example, the chemistry of sand grains trapped in the caulking of the boat planks suggests that the boat was built in Scandinavia and brought across to Orkney on a cargo ship. But even modern excavation could not yield all

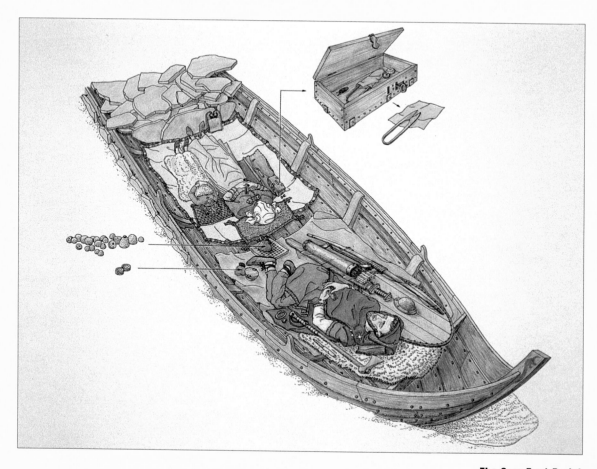

The Scar Boat Burial
Reconstruction drawing of the Scar boat burial.
HISTORIC SCOTLAND / CHRISTINA UNWIN

the secrets of the Scar grave. We do not know, for example, the relationship between these three people – were they mother, son and grandchild; matriarch, warrior kinsman and slave; or some other combination?

There is an impression that the Scar assemblage overall might reflect the height of pagan culture in Viking Orkney, while not being contemporary with it, almost as if the grave reflects the burial the woman might have wished for, had she died when expected by the standards of the time – 20, 30, 40 or more years earlier. If this burial was indeed a late gesture to the old gods and customs of the homelands, this might explain why some aspects of the assemblage seem 'odd', and why some common items appear to be missing. It also raises the unpalat-

able possibility that, when this old woman finally died, two companions were sacrificed to accompany her to the grave – for we do not know how they died. Since all three bodies were buried at once, they probably died within a few hours or days of each other. Perhaps they were struck down by disease, or drowned? And where did they come from? The plaque most probably came from the far north of Norway, in the Troms area. So did this woman travel from within the Norwegian Arctic Circle to Orkney? How long was she in Orkney before she died?

Sometimes, for all our science, we can but marvel at the wealth and variety of the Viking graves, and the strength and strangeness – at least to us – of the pagan beliefs which underpinned them.

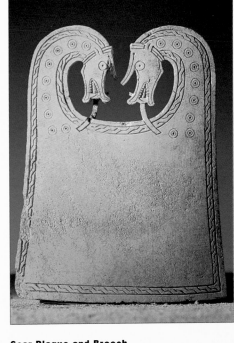

Scar Plaque and Brooch
This magnificent whalebone plaque was probably made in northern Norway and might have been used for pressing pleats or small linen items, such as a cap. The Scar plaque is the finest plaque to have been discovered anywhere in the Viking world. The gilded equal-armed brooch is a rare type of Viking brooch. Strangely, there is no evidence that the Scar woman wore the much more common oval brooches.
HISTORIC SCOTLAND

The Boat
The emptied boat. The clinker-built rowing boat was originally 7.15m long. It was built mainly of oak, but probably had a pine washrail to which the rowlocks were attached. The yellow pins mark the findspots of over 300 iron fastenings.
HISTORIC SCOTLAND

Signpost with Scandinavian Name
Place-names in Orkney are almost entirely
Scandinavian in origin, as seen here on a
present-day signpost.
RICHARD WELSBY, STROMNESS

SOCIETY AND *THING* PLACES

We know how completely the Vikings took over the Northern
Isles by the almost total domination of Scandinavian place-names
in the landscape. Norse land-division was initially based on farms
and fields created by the native population; but the division of
land was gradually developed by succeeding generations of
settlers, who superimposed Norwegian names wholesale. And in
the farm-names of Orkney especially (Shetland may have been a
less aristocratic society), we see a sophisticated system of social
stratification – the different names for 'farm' reflecting a hierarchy
based on their size, location and status.

Skáli names (e.g. Skaill, Langskaill), for example, seem to
apply to later farms with a high-status hall; while *Bu of* names (Bu
of Rapness) were of even higher status, the principal properties of
the earls of Orkney. *Staðir* farm-names (Tormiston, Tenston) are
often joined to personal names and were perhaps the homes of
self-contained individuals of some standing. Many farm-names
end in -bister (Kirbister, Rennibister), from *bólstaðr*, because *ból*
means 'a portion' and was frequently used when home-fields
were divided, especially to form multi-tenanted townships (or
extended farms) surrounding a *Bu of*, or central place. Elsewhere
we see farms developing where there was originally a field (*kví*,
akr: Quoy), an enclosure (*garth*: Garth) or a grazing place (*sætr*:
Setter). By the Late Norse period, and probably earlier, there was
a relationship between place-names and *urislands* (ouncelands),
the 18-penny districts on which *skat* (tax) was paid. Farms were
assessed as whole urislands or regular fractions of urislands (e.g. 9,
4½, 12, 3 pennylands, where a pennyland was land valued at a
penny a year).

This system of land-ownership, administration, and even
semi-democratic representation, is one of the most impressive
aspects of Norse civilisation in the islands. A legal structure was
established probably from the earliest days of settlement, echoing
that of the homelands. A *thing* site (*thing-vollr* [Tingwall], assembly
field) was where judicial and other matters were settled between
individuals, families and chieftains. The Law Ting Holm at
Tingwall was the meeting place of the annual *lawthing*, or parliament, in Shetland, and remained in use into the sixteenth century. People attending the assembly would put up temporary huts
and booths at the end of the fertile Tingwall valley, in the 'Bay of
Huts' (Skálarvagr); these are the origins of the village of
Scalloway, which remained Shetland's capital until the 1600s.
Later on, there were also regional *thing* districts, at Aiths**ting**,
Nes**ting**, and Del**ting**, for example.

There is nothing in Orkney to compare with the impressive
Law Ting Holm in Shetland; the only identifiable Orcadian *thing*

The Viking use of steatite (soapstone)

Steatite, commonly known as soapstone, is a very soft rock, easily carved with metal tools, and was used by the Vikings to make cooking vessels, loomweights, spindle whorls, net sinkers, lamps and other objects. Steatite objects are ubiquitous on Norse settlements – so much so that its presence on sites where the interface between Pictish and Viking levels is blurred, or even where there are no obvious Norse structures, is often used to indicate an otherwise elusive Norse presence. At the beginning of the Viking period, steatite was probably brought in from Western Norway. Later on, the Vikings extensively quarried the steatite outcrops in Shetland, at Clibberswick in Unst and Cunningsburgh on mainland Shetland.

The impressions of Norse bowls are clearly visible in exposed rock faces on either side of the Catpund Burn at Cunningsburgh, where recent excavations have also revealed massive heaps of discarded steatite, the waste left behind after open-cast quarrying and preliminary working of the stone. The Norse in the Orkney earldom relied on vessels of steatite, stone and wood, and did not make use of pottery until the Late Norse period. Even then, their pottery was a soft coarse ware, tempered with grass and unlikely to last long in use.

Cunningsburgh Steatite Quarry, Shetland

The Cunningsburgh steatite quarry, Shetland. The technique was to carve the outside of the bowl upside down, while it was still attached to the rockface, and then to sever it from the face and hollow out the interior.

OLWYN OWEN

Selection of Steatite Objects

Steatite vessels. Small round bowls occur in all periods, while oval ones were used mostly in the tenth and eleventh century. The square ones became popular in the eleventh century. Steatite was also used to make line sinkers, lamps and loom weights.

HISTORIC SCOTLAND

is surprisingly not at Birsay, but at Tingwall in Rendall, in north-east Mainland. Perhaps the authority of the earl prevented this system of fixed local assemblies from thriving in Orkney? The most obvious *thing* site in northern Scotland, to judge from its name, is at Dingwall, at the head of the Cromarty Firth.

The Law Ting Holm, Shetland

The Law Ting Holm juts into an inland loch in the centre of Shetland, a site easily reached overland or from the harbour at Scalloway. There are still traces of a causeway and circular stone enclosure where the *thing* actually met. People waited by the loch shore before being called on to the holm to state their case. The sound of pronouncements would have carried across the water.

HISTORIC SCOTLAND

Pagan Viking graves: a matter of life and death

The early Norse settlers worshipped pagan gods such as Odin, Thor and Freyja. Pagan Viking graves were often richly accompanied by goods, buried to accompany the dead people on their journey to the afterlife. The pagan graves are arguably the most dramatic of archaeological finds from the Orkney earldom, and indeed from all parts of 'Viking Scotland', and bring alive the alien culture of the Vikings even more than their settlements. All the Scottish pagan Viking graves seem to date from about AD 850–950, which accords well with what little we

know of the creation of the earldom of Orkney. From the later tenth century, the Norse settlers began to adopt Christianity and Christian burial customs, after which it becomes difficult to tell the difference between Viking graves and those of any other ethnic group.

In 1963, a farm worker at Westness, on Rousay, Orkney, was burying a dead cow when he chanced upon the grave of a Viking woman and her twin babies, buried in an oval pit lined with flagstones. The woman, who had been rather fat when she was alive, was buried with a lavish selection of grave goods, including the famous Westness brooch. Some forty graves have been excavated at Westness since then, although only eight contained Norse grave goods. Two were boat burials, each containing the body of a single man richly accompanied by weapons and tools. A massive, boat-shaped stone setting nearby contained no burial and may have been a cenotaph.

This cemetery included a wide range of grave types – rectangular cists, stone-lined oval pits, boat-shaped graves, boat burials, shallow rectangular pits, graves with and without goods; and contained men, women and children, from tiny infants to relatively old people aged about 50. All the graves were burials of unburnt bodies (Viking cremations are rare in Scotland), and must originally have been marked by wooden markers or low cairns because later graves did not cut through earlier graves.

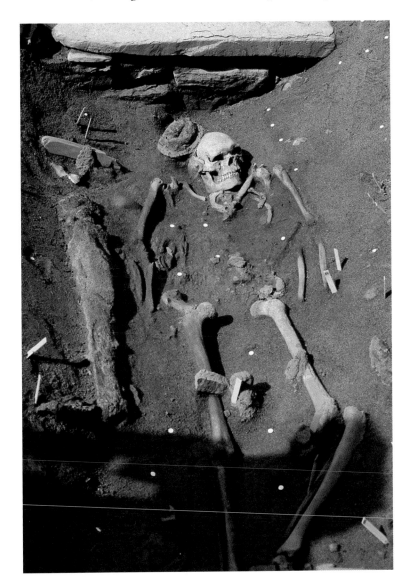

Westness Boat Burial
A tall Viking warrior was buried in a wooden rowing boat in the Westness cemetery, with his sword, shield, axe and other equipment.
OLWYN OWEN

**The
Westness Woman**

The first grave found at
Westness contained a rather fat,
very wealthy woman and her
newborn twin babies: perhaps she died
in childbirth? She was buried with a
wealth of equipment and jewellery –
most important of all, a very fine Celtic
brooch which was perhaps more than a
century old when it was buried. This is
how the Westness woman might have
looked when she was alive (above).
Analysis of her bones suggests that she
often carried a heavy weight on her back
– perhaps in a basket or *caisie*, like this
nineteenth-century Orcadian woman
carrying the peats home (below).
DAVID SIMON

Some of the unaccompanied
burials are certainly pre-
Viking; the Norse settlers
clearly re-used an earlier
Christian, presumably Pictish,
burial ground, though
whether for religious or
political motives is not
known. Others might be
Norse Christian burials; or
unaccompanied for other
reasons, ranging from poverty,
lack of status, lack of regard for
the dead person or simple
meanness. Such speculations are
never clear-cut. For instance, it
is perfectly possible that the first
waves of settlers were followed
by others, who – born and bred in
Norway – arrived as pagans when
Christianity was already taking root
among the Norse in the Northern Isles.
Pagan Viking graves, singly and in
groups, are known from several other sites in
the Northern Isles; but, altogether, there are
perhaps fewer than expected. It is particularly surprising how few
graves are known from Shetland, although two have been found
in Unst. A Christian Norse presence might be inferred from the
discovery of two east-to-west aligned wooden coffins, radiocarbon dated to around the tenth century, at Kebister, Shetland
Mainland. In Caithness there is evidence for a Viking cemetery at
Reay, again recovered haphazardly many years ago, with at least
three pagan graves. Altogether in Caithness and Sutherland,
pagan Viking graves are known from at least seven sites.

Prime areas of Viking settlement in the Orkney earldom will
continue to reveal Viking graves – pagan and Christian – every
now and then. In 1991, for instance, the remarkable burial of a
12 to 14 year old boy was discovered in sand dunes at Balnakeil,
Sutherland. The boy was buried with full-sized adult weapons – a
sword too big for him to have used easily, and a spear and shield
which seem to have been set up as canopy over his head; together with many other objects. Traces of feathers and straw on
his sword suggest that the Balnakeil boy was laid out on straw
matting, with a feather pillow under his head.

The Viking West

Conquest and co-existence

The Annals of Ulster starkly report the first Norse raids at the end of the eighth century: 'The Hebrides and Ireland were plundered by the heathen.' But the islands were conquered, according to the sagas, by the Viking leader Ketil Flat-nose, probably around 850: 'Having landed in the west, Ketil ... conquered and took charge of the Hebrides, making peace alliances with all the leading men there.' It is always difficult to know how much we can rely on saga evidence, but the problems are greater in the Western Isles, for we do not know what peoples these 'leading men' led. The Dál Riata Gaels were probably installed in the southern Inner Hebrides, but the shadowy peoples of eighth- and ninth-century Skye and the Outer Hebrides were peripheral to the world of the Picts, and closer to Scottic and Irish influences.

To the Norwegians, these distinctions probably meant little. The Vikings did not object to mingling with local populations, taking native wives, and swapping allegiances between competing groups when it was in their interests. And there is some support for the notion of 'peace alliances' in contemporary Irish annals. By the mid ninth century, the presence of a Viking-led warrior force of *Gall-Gaedhil*,

Eigg Boat Stem

The discovery of a Viking boat stem buried in a bog on Eigg is somehow symbolic of the Vikings' maritime dominion which paid no heed to territorial boundaries. The boat stem has recently been radiocarbon dated to around the tenth century.

NATIONAL MUSEUMS OF SCOTLAND

Map of the Viking West

To the Norwegians, the western islands – reached by turning south at Cape Wrath (from Old Norse *hvarf*, turning point) – were simply the *Suðreyjar*, Southern Isles, as opposed to the *Norðreyjar*, Northern Isles.

ROB BURNS

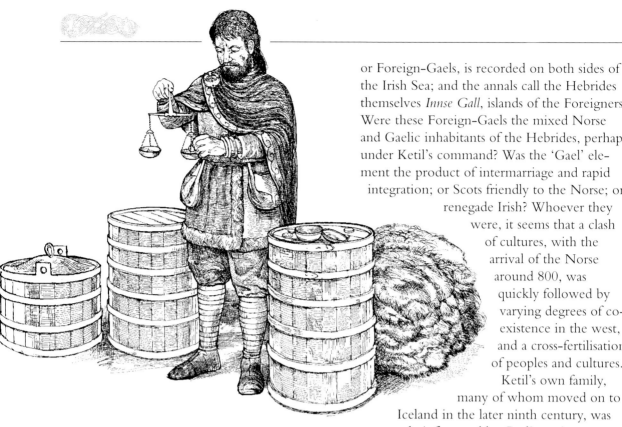

or Foreign-Gaels, is recorded on both sides of the Irish Sea; and the annals call the Hebrides themselves *Innse Gall*, islands of the Foreigners. Were these Foreign-Gaels the mixed Norse and Gaelic inhabitants of the Hebrides, perhaps under Ketil's command? Was the 'Gael' element the product of intermarriage and rapid integration; or Scots friendly to the Norse; or renegade Irish? Whoever they were, it seems that a clash of cultures, with the arrival of the Norse around 800, was quickly followed by varying degrees of co-existence in the west, and a cross-fertilisation of peoples and cultures. Ketil's own family, many of whom moved on to Iceland in the later ninth century, was strongly influenced by Gaelic society, notably in the adoption of Christianity; while links between the Hebrides and Ireland, especially Dublin, were always strong. Ketil's daughter married Olaf, king of Dublin – the same Olaf who, in 870, triumphed after a four-month siege of Dumbarton Rock, capital of the Strathclyde Britons.

Viking Trader
A reconstruction drawing of a Viking trader weighing out hacksilver and ring-money on his portable scales.
DAVID SIMON

Silver Hoard from Storr Rock, Skye
The silver hoard from Storr Rock, Skye, contained over 100 Anglo-Saxon and Arabic coins and some hack-silver. It was originally buried in the ground about AD 935, and is the earliest dated Scandinavian hoard in Scotland.
NATIONAL MUSEUMS OF SCOTLAND

Ring-money
Typical Norse ring-money and two finger-rings from a hoard found at Dibadale, Barvas, Isle of Lewis. Ring-money was a form of currency peculiar to the British Isles, with the rings conforming to an approximate weight standard of about 24g +/− 0.8g.
NATIONAL MUSEUMS OF SCOTLAND

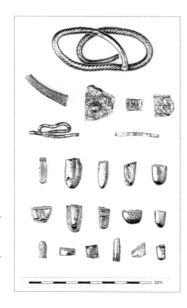

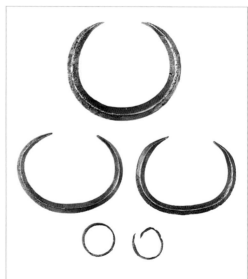

There were strong links, too, between the Outer Hebrides and the Isle of Man, which was the political centre of power in the islands; and, for a short period in the late tenth and early eleventh century, the Hebrides came under the control of the earls of Orkney.

Unlike the Orkney earldom, the Western Isles were never under the permanent control of one Norse family and remained the domain of warlords. There were many bidders for their services, given the important strategic position of the islands along this western axis. A struggle for power in Hebridean waters is reflected by a cluster of Viking silver hoards, all buried for safekeeping in the area in the 980s. These include a savings-hoard from Iona which might have been brought to the monastery by Olaf Sihtricsson, the penitent Norse king of Dublin, who retired there in 980. His presence did not deter the raiders: ironically, on Christmas night in 986, Iona was plundered yet again.

When, in 1014, Earl Sigurd of Orkney gathered a formidable fleet of warships to fight with the king of Dublin against Brian Boru, king of Munster, his warriors included men from Orkney, Shetland, Man, Skye, Lewis, Kintyre and Argyll. It was not just loyalty to Sigurd that brought together this great force. The common interest of these scattered islanders and coastal dwellers was the protection of Norse power and influence in Ireland – the main source of their wealth along the sea road.

As in the north, the Viking Age silver hoards reveal a picture of great wealth accruing in the islands from about the middle of the tenth century onwards. Most hoards were buried in the later tenth and eleventh centuries. Every so often, another one is found. In 1988, over 40 pieces of hack-silver, wrapped in linen cloth and then placed in a cattle horn, were found in the grounds of Lews Castle, Stornoway, where they had been buried about 990–1040. As in the Orkney earldom, their contents reflect strong connections with the Irish Sea area, and ring-money is a common occurrence.

Graves in the Western Isles and the question of ethnicity

Until recently, Viking graves in the west seemed mostly to comprise individual, often especially wealthy, burials. Substantial burial mounds have also only been securely identified in the west, as at Kiloran Bay, Colonsay, and on the Isle of Man. This seemed to imply that the 'best' graves, and therefore the richest and most important Vikings, lived in the west. We now know this assumption to be flawed, but let us look first at one or two of these great western burials.

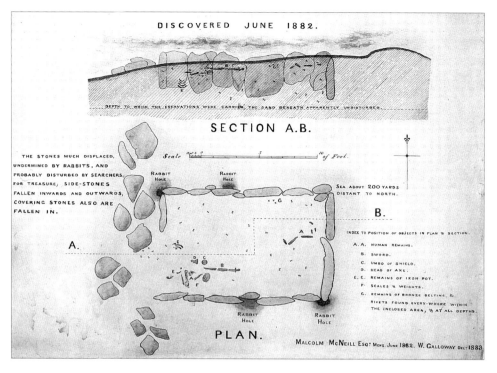

Kiloran Bay Original Excavation Plan

The original excavation plan of the Kiloran Bay burial, excavated in 1882.

ROYAL COMMISSION ON ANCIENT AND HISTORICAL MONUMENTS OF SCOTLAND

Selection of Kiloran Bay Artefacts

Finds from the Kiloran Bay, Colonsay, burial included balance scales and this set of lead weights ornamented with scraps of Celtic or Anglo-Saxon metalwork. There was also a complete set of weapons (sword, spearhead, axe, shield and arrowheads); an iron-handled pot, sickle, knife and whetstone; bronze pins and bronze mountings for a harness.

NATIONAL MUSEUMS OF SCOTLAND

At Kiloran Bay, Colonsay, a powerfully built, middle-aged man was buried within a rectangular stone-built enclosure, the whole apparently covered by an inverted boat, with a mound of sand on top. Buried with him was a horse, and an exceptional assemblage of Scandinavian and Insular grave goods. Three Anglo-Saxon coins tell us that the grave dates to no earlier than the mid ninth century. The Kiloran Bay grave is reminiscent of several great ninth-century Isle of Man graves. Like them, it is thought to be that of a wealthy 'aristocratic' pagan Scandinavian settler; and yet, two of the enclosure slabs are crudely carved with Christian crosses — evidence of someone aware of another religious tradition and 'hedging his bets' in death.

Two other burials from Colonsay come from the Machrins dunes in an area whose name, Cnoc nan Gall, means 'hillock of the foreigners'. One was a rich male burial; in the second a woman was buried with her lap dog, which had its head on the woman's knees. This grave was disturbed by rabbits but, intriguingly, none of the surviving grave goods are demonstrably Scandinavian. The grave is nonetheless indisputably pagan.

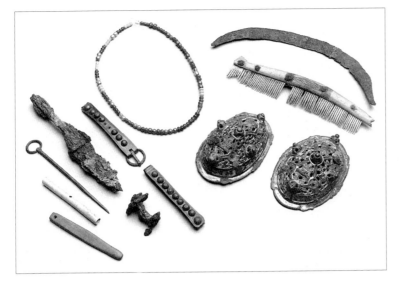

Valtos Grave Goods

Selection of grave goods from a wealthy grave at Cnip, Valtos, found in 1979. (see overleaf)

NATIONAL MUSEUMS OF SCOTLAND

Many of the Western Isles graves were found in the nineteenth century and the accounts are confused. From Oronsay, there may have been another boat burial in a mound, perhaps containing the richly accompanied bodies of an elderly man and two women. The records are better for the Ballinaby cemetery on Islay, where at least three wealthy graves were found. Two male burials were lavishly accompanied by weapons, and one included blacksmithing tools, a hammer and forge tongs, and the terminal from a drinking horn. A wealthy female grave is comparable to that of the Scar woman in its textile implements; but she also had typical Viking oval brooches, elaborate bronze mountings, a silver dress pin and safety chain, twelve beads and a bronze ladle. Early accounts tell of many other human bones and weapons from this vicinity, all now lost.

The famous Hebridean (and Isle of Man) pagan graves give the impression of being those of aristocratic Norsemen – of higher status than those in the north. But recent discoveries of more modest graves in the Western Isles are qualifying this picture – just as the Westness cemetery, the Scar boat burial and the Balnakeil boy have provided new 'benchmarks' in northern Scotland. In fact, it is unlikely that early Viking settlers in Orkney were any less wealthy, generally speaking, than those in the west. The reasons for any differences in burial type and ritual are not economic, but cultural and political; they reflect the differing nature and development of Viking colonisation and settlement in western and northern Scotland. And this was dictated, at least in part, by the varying degrees of vigour and persistence of native cultures, the sheer numbers of existing inhabitants, and the speed (or otherwise) with which Viking settlers assimilated, or were assimilated into, native culture.

Viking settlers were also converted to Christianity at variable rates, in different areas of Scotland. Traditionally it has been argued that, since pagan Viking graves are accompanied by goods, then unaccompanied graves cannot be Viking. But Christian graves give little indication of the ethnic origins of the deceased (as we saw at Westness), and it is highly probable that some unaccompanied graves, at known Viking burial locations or in areas of Viking settlement, are actually the graves of Viking settlers. Conversely, some unaccompanied graves, even in Viking burial locations, probably contain the bodies of members of the native Celtic population. Viking period radiocarbon dates cannot identify the race or religion of the deceased.

A 'hybrid' cemetery at Cnip, Valtos, Lewis

The conundrum of unaccompanied graves is amply demonstrated in the Cnip cemetery, where, of seven graves examined since 1979, only four are demonstrably Viking – accompanied by Viking grave goods – and only one of those was richly equipped. The wealthy grave was that of a 35–40 year old woman, buried in typical Viking dress and wearing oval brooches, a necklace of 44 glass beads, a ringed pin, bronze belt-buckle and strap-end. She also had some useful implements with her: an iron knife and whetstone; a sickle; and a bone needle case with two iron needles.

Nearby was a cluster of another five burials: three adults, one infant and a new-born baby, all buried in shallow pits; and another child burial was found a little upslope. The adult graves – two men and one woman – were marked by low mounds, surrounded by rectangular arrangements of stones. The woman had a bone pin and perforated iron pin at her shoulder. The infant wore a necklace of amber beads and its clothing had been secured by a fine bone pin; while the other child had an amber bead and pendant, both presumably worn round the neck. The other graves were unaccompanied and it is not clear whether they are

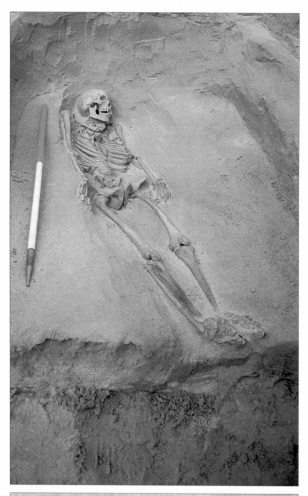

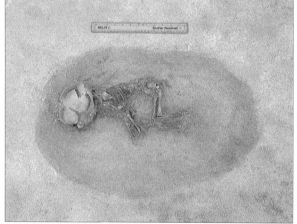

those of Scandinavians or not.

Another wealthy female burial, discovered in 1916, but described only as 'from Valtos', may also have belonged to this cemetery; and it is highly likely that further graves will be revealed as the sand dunes continue to erode. In the meantime, what are we to make of this strange mix of associated graves – unaccompanied, poorly accompanied and richly accompanied? Clearly, one possibility is that we are seeing the varying cultural and religious affiliations present in ninth- and tenth-century Lewis. Analysis of the human bone assemblage has confirmed that life was hard for all the Viking Age inhabitants: they endured poor conditions during childhood and arduous working conditions in later life. Both men had suffered broken bones; at least one skeleton had a spinal injury; and infant mortality was obviously high.

Recently Excavated Graves at Cnip
The excavated graves of an adult and a small child at Cnip.
HISTORIC SCOTLAND

Lewis
A typical view of the landscape of the Western Isles, as it would have greeted the arrival of the Vikings.
HISTORIC SCOTLAND

Viking settlements in the west

The Norse-Gaelic intermingling in the Western Isles is also evident in the place-names. Scandinavian names are everywhere in the landscape, including *staðir*, *sætr* and *bólstaðr* – indicating settlement. But the proportion of Norse to Gaelic names varies from north to south, and from the Outer Hebrides to the Inner. Of 126 village names in Lewis, for instance, 99 are purely Scandinavian, and there is a large percentage of Scandinavian names in Skye; but only 10% of settlement names in Rhum, Eigg and Canna are Norse. The picture is not clear-cut because of the over-laying of Gaelic names after the Viking period.

Against this background, it has always seemed strange that, until recently, few Viking settlements were known in the Hebrides: a long-lived domestic settlement at the Udal, North Uist; a single farm at Drimore, South Uist; and a settlement at Little Dunagoil, Bute. At the Udal, the story is again one of characteristic Norse rectangular buildings, with their central long hearths, being built over the ruins of an earlier native settlement.

In the 1990s, a scatter of Norse settlements has been identified in the Bhaltos area of Lewis. At Barvas, environmental evidence from the middens suggests that the economic basis of the farmstead was similar to that of Norse farms in Orkney. Barley and oats were the staple crops, with some flax; cattle and sheep were the

Eigg Sword Hilt
Amongst the finds from probably three graves discovered in substantial mounds on Eigg is a magnificent late eighth- or ninth-century Norwegian sword hilt. Several other poorly recorded graves are known from other islands: Barra, Eriskay and South Uist.
NATIONAL MUSEUMS OF SCOTLAND

dominant animal breeds, with small quantities of pig, red deer and horse; while the fish remains were mainly cod, ling and saithe. Most calves were killed shortly after birth,

Arnol Blackhouse, Lewis

The blackhouses of the Western Isles continued a tradition stretching back a thousand years, with the dwelling and byre built under one roof. The Arnol blackhouse, pictured here, was built as late as 1885.

HISTORIC SCOTLAND

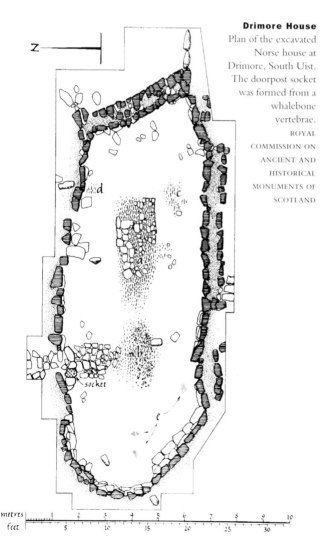

Drimore House
Plan of the excavated Norse house at Drimore, South Uist. The doorpost socket was formed from a whalebone vertebrae.
ROYAL COMMISSION ON ANCIENT AND HISTORICAL MONUMENTS OF SCOTLAND

encouraging milk production by their mothers, which suggests (not surprisingly given the landscape) that dairying was more important here than in the Northern Isles. Sheep were often kept for two summers and could also have produced milk. Otters were hunted for their pelts. Occasional whalebones show that stranded whales were exploited.

More exciting still is the discovery of more than 20 Viking Age settlement mounds along the machair on the west coast of South Uist. At last we may be seeing the true scale and nature of Viking Age settlement in parts of the Western Isles. Research and excavations at two of these sites, Kilphedir and Bornish, are gradually building up a picture of settlement across a locality.

The political end-game in the west

By around 1150, Somerled mac Gille-Brigde, a Celto-Norse ruler in Argyll, was carving out a power base in areas which were previously part of the Norse kingdom of Man and the Isles, dependent on the king of Norway. In 1156, Somerled succeeded in wresting control of all the *Suðreyjar* south of Ardnamurchan Point, from the king of Man. Somerled's successes marked the beginning of a Celtic resurgence which culminated in the emergence of the Lordship of the Isles, although Somerled himself was killed at the hands of Malcolm IV's troops in 1164.

Somerled's death allowed the Scottish king to extend his authority into the coastal areas of Argyll and the Clyde estuary although, for the time being, all the Hebrides remained subject to Norway. It was during this period that one of the most remarkable finds from Norse Scotland was buried in the ground – the famous Lewis chessmen. Seventy-eight elaborately carved figures – or the greater part of four chess sets – together with 14 plain

Rothesay Castle
Rothesay castle on Bute was besieged and taken by Norsemen in 1230, who hacked at the wall with axes and breached it. It was briefly captured again during King Hakon's invasion of the west in 1263.
HISTORIC SCOTLAND

draughtsmen and a belt buckle, all of walrus ivory, were found in 1831, hidden in a stone cist in sand dunes at Uig Bay. The decoration on these valuable items suggests that they were made in Norway. We can only wonder what strange circumstances led to them being buried in a remote spot on Lewis.

By the thirteenth century, the tide of history was running against the Norwegians in the west. In 1230, they briefly captured Rothesay Castle, Bute, from the Scots, but withdrew shortly afterwards to Kintyre. In 1263, King Haakon IV of Norway personally led a final, doomed attempt to re-take Bute and Kintyre from Alexander III, king of Scots. As in the old days, Haakon's fleet gathered support from the Celto-Norse inhabitants of the Western Isles and Islay as it made its way south; but with the weather worsening, and after an inconclusive confrontation at Largs, the Norwegians retreated again. Haakon himself died on the way home, at Kirkwall in Orkney. Three years later, by the Treaty of Perth, his son Magnus finally handed over the kingdom of Man and the Isles to the Scottish king – in return for 4000 marks and an annual payment of 100 marks 'for ever'. The Viking west was over.

The Kilphedir and Bornish settlements, South Uist

Kilphedir
A general view of the
virgin location of the
Kilphedir settlement.
HISTORIC SCOTLAND/
UNIVERSITY OF SHEFFIELD

The settlement at Kilphedir lay hidden beneath more than 2m of sand and was only revealed as the sand cliff eroded into the sea. Rescue excavations have uncovered a sequence of eleven buildings, including five stone-built longhouses. Altogether, the settlement was in use for some 300 years, from around 1000 until 1300. Unlike the Udal (and, indeed, unlike other newly found Viking settlements in South Uist), the first longhouse was erected on undisturbed sand, and not on the remains of any pre-Viking settlement; even though, interestingly, the nearest Iron Age settlement mound is only 500 metres away.

One of the very first structures was of wood, but the inhabitants mainly built their houses in stone and turf. Although the houses were

typically Norse in form – long and roughly rectangular with central hearths – they copied the Hebridean tradition of sunken-floored dwellings with single-faced stone walls holding back the sand. Only one longhouse was in use at any one time, together with either an attached or detached square out-house, suggesting that this was the farm of a single family. Each time a new longhouse was built, the old house was dismantled, but its lowest courses were partly re-used as the foundations for the new house. Each new house was constructed with its long axis at right angles to that of its immediate predecessor, so that the houses 'criss-cross' each other in chronological sequence. The small outhouses do not seem to have been byres as they each had a hearth; they might have been used for baking, brewing or crop-processing.

The second earliest stone-built house was over 14m long with

rounded corners and slightly bowed walls, and had a cobbled forecourt. Its main dwelling room was over 10m long, with a central hearth, and was connected by a short passage to another small squarish room, which also had a hearth. Both rooms had layers of floor deposits and produced a variety of artefacts including bone pins, an almost complete comb, a glass bead and two bone crucifix pendants. Later on the house was reduced in size by the insertion of a partition wall, which also cut off access to the smaller room. An English green-glazed tripod pitcher from the floor, and a coin of King Cnut (1016–1035) found in the later levels, date abandonment of this house to around the mid twelfth century.

Two smaller stone-walled structures were built next, at right angles to and on top of the aban-doned longhouse. One was probably an outhouse; but the other had occupation layers, and a niche in its wall contained large fragments of pottery platters. One of the things which distinguishes Viking material culture in the Western Isles from that in the north is the use of pottery, as well as steatite vessels. Hebridean Viking Age pottery mainly comprises undecorated flat-based bowls and platters, often grass-impressed, and is quite different from any pottery previously in use in the Hebrides. This pottery type was first identified at the Udal but is now known from many sites, and from as far south as Tiree.

These Kilphedir structures were replaced by another fine Norse longhouse, over 8m long internally and up to 4m wide, one end of which may have been partitioned off by a wooden screen. Amongst many other things, its hearth and floor levels

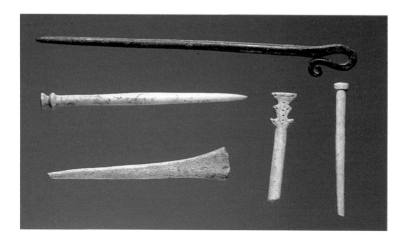

Bornish Finds
A selection of bone and
metal pins from Bornish.
HISTORIC SCOTLAND/
UNIVERSITY OF SHEFFIELD

produced a strip of silver, a whale-bone flax paddle, finely executed bone pins, flints, whetstones and crude gaming counters. Midden deposits which had accumulated around the building also produced a rich assemblage of finds and environmental evidence.

The final longhouse was smaller than the others, about 7m long inside, with relatively straight walls, a 4m long central hearth, and with two opposing doorways in its long walls reached by narrow passages from outside the building. A short-cross penny of King John of England (1199–1216) from its upper layers provides an end date for the settlement. The assemblages from Kilphedir clearly show Hebridean involvement in the Viking world, with English pottery and coins, and Shetland steatite, all recovered from this family farm.

At Bornish, some 10km to the north, geophysical survey and trial excavations on three settlement mounds have revealed the most extensive and complex Norse settlement so far discovered in the Western Isles – about 20 buildings covering an area of some 0.8 hectares. The artefacts are of similar quality to those from Kilphedir, but there is a significant difference in the animal remains. Cattle, sheep and pig were being raised at both sites, but much more venison was being consumed at Bornish than at Kilphedir. The excavators have suggested that herds of red deer were being managed and maintained in South Uist – perhaps specifically for hunting, which was often an activity of the higher levels of society.

Bornish was occupied for longer than Kilphedir, probably into the early 1300s, but then it too was abandoned. By now the inhabitants were the product of centuries of cultural and ethnic intermingling. For some reason, these medieval Hebrideans opted to leave the fertile machair that had sustained their Norse, Celtic and prehistoric ancestors for thousands of years, and moved inland to the edge of the blacklands.

The Allure of the Lowlands

All too often, the dramatic story of the Vikings in the far north and west eclipses their role in the Scottish lowlands, where the tangled tale of the emerging Scottish nation was being played out. In fact, the Vikings had a profound impact on the history of both Scotland and England in the ninth and tenth centuries. Indeed, it was partly the struggles of established groupings *against* Scandinavians that prompted the emergence of unified kingdoms in both countries. For much of the period the kings of Scots found themselves 'encircled' by Vikings – Norwegians to north and west, and Danes to the south in England – and cut their political cloth accordingly. In the 860s, for example, the Scottish king, Constantine I, connived in the Norse king of Dublin's campaigns against the Picts and the Strathclyde Britons; but was himself killed in battle against the Danes in 877.

By the tenth century, the emergence of a Danish Viking kingdom based in York and the entrenchment of Norse kings in Dublin had given rise to a powerful Scandinavian axis in early medieval Britain – based on commerce and backed up by deft political manoeuvrings. The co-operation of the Scots, whether by alliance or subjugation, was essential to maintain lines of communication. For the Vikings, one allure of the lowlands may have been the Firths of Forth and Clyde – potentially a major route linking York and Dublin. Recent experiments have shown that Viking boats could be carried, dragged or rolled on timbers across some considerable distance overland, from one waterway to another.

In the tenth century there was a long period of collaboration between the Scots and the Dublin–York Scandinavians. King Constantine II (900–943) married his daughter to Olaf Guthfrithsson of Dublin, and even gave his eldest son a Scandinavian name – Indulf, king of Scots from 954 to 962. Such close dynastic links must have created an environment friendly to Scandinavians; and a scatter of Scandinavian place-names suggests a sparse but permanent presence in southern and eastern Scotland. Throughout the Viking Age, Scandinavians and peoples of Anglo- and Celto-Scandinavian descent encroached into the Scottish lowlands and left tell-tale cultural markers – not only place-names, but also silver hoards and sculpture.

Comb from Dunbar, East Lothian
Viking finds sometimes turn up in strange places. Two typical Viking combs of the early ninth or tenth century were found on an Anglian settlement at Castle Park, Dunbar; and another Viking comb was discovered recently in soil removed from the graveyard of the old parish church in North Berwick, both in east Lothian.
HISTORIC SCOTLAND / SCOTTISH URBAN ARCHAEOLOGICAL TRUST

Portage of Viking Boats
Modern experiments have shown that Viking boats could be dragged or rolled considerable distances overland from one navigable waterway to another. This is one reason why the Vikings were able to penetrate up the river systems so far into eastern Europe.
DAVID MACCULLOUGH

The Viking hogbacks

One of the stranger legacies of the Vikings in northern Britain is the hogback tombstone, found only in northern England and southern Scotland. These extraordinary three-dimensional, house-shaped sculptures, with their distinctive curved 'roof' ridges, were a tenth-century invention of the Norse-Irish settlers in northern Yorkshire. Hogbacks in Scotland mostly occur close to maritime routes, especially around the estuaries of the Clyde and Forth. An early example comes from the island of Inchcolm, actually in the Firth of Forth.

Most hogbacks have Christian connections; and, in fact, all major ecclesiastical sites in eastern Scotland have produced a hogback stone. The Anglo-Scandinavian patrons of the hogback carvers were clearly at home in a Christian setting, but does this mean that there were permanent Scandinavian settlements on the doorsteps of these ecclesiastical sites? The enigmatic hogbacks have little to say on this score.

GOVAN IN THE KINGDOM OF STRATHCLYDE

A group of five Scottish hogbacks from Govan Old parish church, on the south bank of the Clyde, are perhaps the most remarkable. These are the largest and heaviest of all hogbacks. One with rudimentary end-beasts is a Cumbrian type, suggesting a maritime connection between the Cumberland settlements and the Clyde estuary. On another, the end-beast is a three-dimensional, full-bodied animal with legs, which appears to straddle the monument. Another is clearly modelled on a Scandinavian house type, with its shingled roof descending almost to the ground.

It is something of a puzzle that Govan was home to a school of stonecarving in the tenth

Dane's Dyke and Constantine's Cave, Fife
Constantine I is reputed to have met his end in Constantine's Cave, Fife Ness, in 877. At around the same time, monks on the Isle of May, just off the coast here, were massacred by Vikings. A large defensive earthwork of unknown date, which cuts off the Ness and cave, is traditionally known as Dane's Dyke.
HEADLAND ARCHAEOLOGY

Inchcolm Hogback
The Inchcolm hogback, found on an island in the Firth of Forth, was once associated with a standing cross, testifying to the Christian connections of these stones. This hogback stone has inward-facing end beasts with muzzles. End beasts are common features on hogback stones. At Meigle, the sculptor has turned the whole monument into a crouching beast.
HISTORIC SCOTLAND

The Viking Age market place at Whithorn

Whithorn occupies an obscure inland site some 5km from the sea, and it is hard to imagine what attracted settlement to this spot until you realise that it was originally a cult centre. The 'cult' was that of St Ninian, and at its centre was the church he built probably in the early fifth century. The early monastery developed and thrived until about 845, when a crisis culminated in the burning of the buildings – which, for once, was probably nothing to do with the Vikings. Before then, life within the enclave was thoroughly Northumbrian, an ecclesiastical community safe within an area of Anglian settlement in south-west Scotland. As the monastery grew in wealth and importance, a thriving market place was kindled on its doorstep, even in this inauspicious location.

So what happened in the Viking period? Well, historical obscurity envelops Whithorn and Galloway after the mid ninth century, just as Scandinavian place-names appear in the landscape; but excavations at Whithorn have given us a fascinating glimpse of a complex cultural evolution. Whithorn survived as an ecclesiastical site, albeit on a smaller scale, and was the home of a distinctive school of sculpture in the tenth century. An alliance may even have been forged between Britons, Angles and Scandinavians to restore the *minster* and preserve its endowments. A new church was built and later demolished. A new settlement of small wattle buildings was erected on higher ground, and another cluster of buildings built over the remains of the church. Later still, in the late tenth or early eleventh century, the settlement was transformed again, with the erection of a densely packed band of small buildings at 45 to the former Northumbrian buildings, enclosed by shallow ditches.

And, by now, the material culture and economy of the settlement was recognisably Norse. There were specifically Norse objects such as a bronze strip decorated with mid eleventh-century Viking animal ornament, and a piece of silver ring-money used as bullion; and objects made at Whithorn by Norse craftsmen, or by Celtic craftsmen for Norse patrons, such as a decorated leather offcut or trial piece, and a board for playing the Viking game of *Hnefatafl*. There was a series of Irish/Norse ring pins spanning the tenth to twelfth centuries, and a fine carved antler handle of the tenth to eleventh century; a small group of Souterrain Ware sherds suggesting the presence of Ulstermen in the settlement; and amber beads testifying to long-range trade with the Baltic. Most important, there was the copious antler waste from the manufacture of Viking combs in workshops – the ubiquitous indicator of a Viking Age town. By the twelfth century, with the market place fully developed, a new style of wattle building was being erected at Whithorn – smaller but otherwise strikingly similar to buildings in Hiberno-Norse Dublin.

This was not a typical Viking town on the Scandinavian model. Galloway lay at a crossroads of Irish, Northumbrian, Scandinavian and British influences, and all are reflected in the assemblages from Whithorn. The Norse were opportunists; the existence of a flourishing centre was all the encouragement they needed to add their voice to the cultural cacophany that was tenth- to twelfth-century Whithorn. And they were pragmatists with clear priorities. If accepting Christianity was the price of being allowed to trade, then so be it.

The Manufacture of Viking combs
A modern experiment in the manufacture of Viking combs. All the tools used would have been available to the Viking comb-makers. The finished comb took about six hours to make and was surprisingly robust.
RAYMOND LAMB/JULIE GIBSON

Cat skull
Found at Whithorn
THE WHITHORN TRUST

Norse Market Place at Whithorn

Reconstruction of Norse workshops in the market place at Whithorn, based on the excavated evidence. A group of discarded cat skulls was found in a pit near the Viking workshops, suggesting that cats were being kept, killed and skinned, presumably for their fur. The craftsmen in the foreground are making antler combs.

DAVID SIMON

and eleventh centuries, producing a rich variety of sculpture including the hogbacks. Govan is only 11 miles upstream from Dumbarton Rock, the old capital of the Strathclyde Britons, which never recovered from its comprehensive sacking by the Vikings in 870. The subsequent fate of the kingdom of Strathclyde is shrouded in mystery. Govan may have become the principal royal centre, with the Strathclyde kings clients of the Scottish kings. But the Govan hogbacks hint also at a close connection between Strathclyde and the Norse – perhaps even at intermarriage between the Strathclyde kings and the Norse dynasty in Man.

The south-west: a cultural crossroads

Galloway, in the far south-west of Scotland, lay at a pivotal point along the Norse sea road – between the Hebrides and the Orkney earldom to the north, and the colonies in Man and Dublin to the south. For years it was assumed that Galloway must have been an important centre of Norse power in Scotland, for it seemed inconceivable that the Vikings would have ignored these strategic shores.

This was despite the meanest of pickings from the ground. Pagan Viking graves, for example, are extremely scarce in the south-west, suggesting little or no colonisation in the early Viking period. Even the discovery of one definite Viking grave, with a sword, penannular brooch and jet bead, is ambivalent – it was found in a Christian churchyard in Kirkcudbright.

We are just beginning to understand that the pattern of Scandinavian involvement here was both subtle and complex. The clearest

Viking Attack on Dumbarton Rock
When King Olaf captured Dumbarton Rock, the capital of the Strathclyde Britons, in 870, there were so many captives, it took a fleet of 200 longships to ferry them to Dublin.
HISTORIC SCOTLAND

Govan Hogbacks
Perhaps the most remarkable Scottish hogbacks are a group of five from Govan Old parish church, on the south bank of the Clyde. This one, with its slim section and formal patterns, probably dates from the mid tenth century and closely resembles hogbacks in Cumbria.
T.E. GRAY

evidence lies in the place-names. Scandinavian names in the south-west show early Viking seafarers thoroughly familiar with the Solway coastline and naming navigational features (e.g. *nes*, a coastal promontory, as in Eggerness; and *holmr*, a low-lying island, as in Estholm). A few name elements show Scandinavians venturing further inland, mostly in Dumfriesshire (e.g. *bekkr*, a stream; *gil*, a ravine; *fjall*, a hill; *dalr*, a valley), one or two of which might denote settlement. Conversely, there are only about 50 actual Scandinavian settlement names in the whole of Dumfries and Galloway, and not a single certain occurrence of *staðir*, *sætr* or *bólstaðr* – the farm-names so common in the Northern and Western Isles. Instead, the most frequent Scandinavian settlement name is *-by* (e.g. Bysbie), especially around the head of the Solway Firth, which was used in Scandinavia and the English Danelaw of any kind of settlement from a small farm to a thriving town. The Danelaw was the name given to that huge swathe of eastern England under Danish control from the ninth century; for a long time, the Danes controlled everywhere north and east of a line drawn from London to Chester.

The picture that emerges is of Scandinavians, most of whose immediate origins probably lay in the English Danelaw, settling in parts of eastern Dumfries-shire, west and north of Kirkcudbright, and in the Whithorn district of Wigtownshire. There is almost nothing to suggest that Scandinavian settlers here came from Norway or the Northern or Western Isles. The sole exception is at Tinwald, Dumfriesshire; only in this *thing* name might we have evidence for a community of Norwegian

Building a Viking Age house at Whithorn
An experiment in building a Norse house at Whithorn, based on the excavated evidence.
THE WHITHORN TRUST

settlers, dominant enough to organise a legal assembly according to their own laws and customs. For the most part, the Norse from areas of Scotland completely under Norwegian control seem to have sailed the sea road right past the south-west. Overall, the place-names

Map of Viking Age southern Scotland
This map shows Scandinavian place-names, hogbacks and silver hoards.

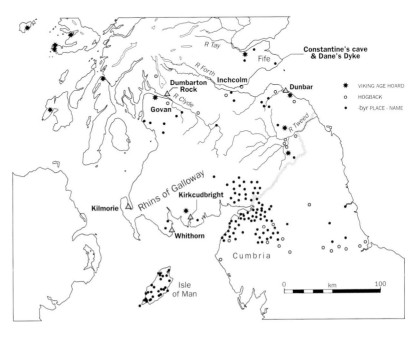

indicate neither a ruling Scandinavian elite, nor a large influx of Scandinavian settlers in the south-west.

Instead, the many non-Scandinavian place-names which survived into medieval times reveal the enduring existence of extensive Northumbrian estates, peopled by Anglian speakers, with the intervening 'blank' areas presumably still occupied by the original British inhabitants. Scandinavian names tend to occur in small pockets within larger blocks of Northumbrian settlement. The place-name evidence smacks of some accommodation between the Scandinavians and their Northumbrian hosts, rather than conquest. Perhaps we should not be surprised at the irony, then, that the most persuasive and illuminating archaeological evidence for Scandinavians in the south-west comes from an important Northumbrian monastic site – at Whithorn, Galloway.

The Kilmorie cross-slab and the story of Sigurd

The Vikings loved a good story, especially if it told of gods, mythical heroes and magic. And scenes from the same stories crop up again and again in Scandinavian art. On one face of the remarkable Kilmorie cross-slab in Galloway, for example, beneath a crude representation of Christ being crucified on a hammer-headed cross, there is another figure, with two stylised birds to the left, and a pair of smith's tongs and possibly an anvil to the right. The imagery of birds and smith's tools conjures up a famous character in Scandinavian mythology – the legendary hero, Sigurd the dragon-slayer.

The dragon was Fafnir, which guarded an ill-gotten hoard of gold. The dragon's brother, Regin the smith, persuaded Sigurd to kill Fafnir with a special sword he had made. On advice from the pagan god Odin, Sigurd hid in a pit and killed the dragon as it passed overhead. Afterwards, Regin asked Sigurd to cook the dragon's heart. When Sigurd did this, he burned his fingers and sucked them, accidentally drinking the heart juices. He was immediately able to understand the language of birds. The birds warned him that Regin intended to kill him and carry off the dragon's treasure on his horse. And so Sigurd beheaded Regin first, and took the gold. But the gold was cursed, of course – and eventually both Sigurd and his brother, Gunnar, came to a sticky end.

The Kilmorie slab and some other tenth- to eleventh-century Viking Age sculptures in northern Britain show how Scandinavian legends could be adapted to a Christian purpose. Like the hogbacks, they reinforce the cultural connection between southern Cumbria, the Galloway peninsula, and the Clyde valley around Govan. The link was along the western sea road.

Kilmorie Slab

One side of the Kilmorie cross-slab. Weland the smith's tongs are clearly visible on this Viking influenced carving.

HISTORIC SCOTLAND

The Orkney Earldom in the Twelfth Century and Later

In many ways, life in the Orkney earldom – still a Norwegian colony – remained unchanged through the twelfth and thirteenth centuries. The population continued to grow. Indeed, population pressures in the eleventh, twelfth and thirteenth centuries strained to its limit the language of naming sub-divisions of land, and generated strange contradictions such as Upper Nisthouse (meaning the upper-lowest house).

The agricultural and economic basis of the islands was similar to that of the earlier Norse period, although fishing became increasingly important. At Freswick and Robertshaven, both in Caithness, massive middens adjacent to Late Norse settlements contain almost nothing but fish bones, as deep-sea fishing and fish-processing became semi-commercialised. Similar middens are also known in the northern islands of Orkney. By the thirteenth century, some places in Orkney and Caithness were engaged in extensive trade in dry-salted fish.

Late Norse houses were more elaborate in plan than those of the earlier period. The living space was reorganised: the long walls were built straighter; long fires were replaced with smaller central fireplaces, or oven-like hearths placed against walls or in room corners; large benches were built along the gable ends of living rooms; and offshooting smaller rooms were added to the main building, usually flanking the central doorways in the long walls.

The material culture remained recognisably Norse, and stayed in tune with the rest of the Scandinavian world as object types and styles

of decoration slowly changed. Objects continued to be imported from Norway, including a different type of steatite used for baking plates. One big change in the Late Norse earldom was that quality pottery began to be imported – from mainland Scotland, England, north Germany and the Low Countries.

Just one god

The single most important change was in religion. By now the Scandinavians were thoroughly Christian and a great spate of church building was underway. We do not know precisely why or how the Vikings in the

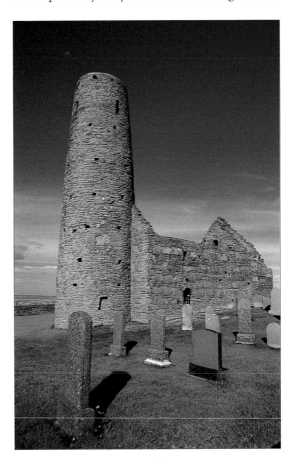

Egilsay Church
Some twenty years after the martyrdom of Magnus in 1117, the beautiful St Magnus Church, Egilsay, with its distinctive round tower, was built on the spot where he died.
HISTORIC SCOTLAND

Cross Kirk, Tuquoy

Norse landowners often built private chapels near their halls or settlements. Their locations signal a developing ecclesiastical network, normally with one chapel per ounceland (a unit of land for tax assessment). Cross Kirk, at Tuquoy, Westray, was originally an ounceland chapel, built next to a high-status stone hall and settlement. In the thirteenth century, it was enlarged to become the parish church. HISTORIC SCOTLAND

earldom adopted Christianity. According to the sagas, in 995 the newly baptised Norwegian king, Olaf Tryggvason, arrived in Orkney and gave Earl Sigurd the Stout a choice: 'I want you and all your subjects to be baptised. If you refuse, I'll have you killed on the spot, and I swear I'll ravage every island with fire and steel.' With wry understatement, the saga says: 'the earl could see what kind of situation he was in', and promptly accepted baptism. Not surprisingly, Sigurd's conversion was at best half-hearted. He died a true Viking – at the head of a great army of Norsemen fighting the Irish at the battle of Clontarf in 1014 – wrapped in the famous raven banner, a symbol of Odin.

Christianity probably only became firmly established over the next few decades. Sigurd's son was the powerful Earl Thorfinn the Mighty, who went on a great European tour and visited the pope in Rome, after which he 'finished with piracy'. Thorfinn is credited with building the first church in Viking Orkney, in about 1050 – at Birsay, the seat of the first

Orkney bishopric. By the twelfth century, most of the important families in the earldom were building chapels on their estates.

The greatest churches were built by the earls, and show that twelfth-century Norse Orkney was in the mainstream of European cultural and artistic development. It was Earl Rognvald who began the building of St Magnus Cathedral, Kirkwall, in 1137, employing only the finest masters and masons from Durham. Nearby was the bishop's palace, where King Haakon of Norway died in 1263 after losing the battle of Largs. The cathedral was named after the saintly Earl Magnus, who was lured to a martyr's death on Egilsay in 1117, by his rival for the earldom, Haakon. Earl Haakon later journeyed to Rome and Jerusalem seeking absolution and, probably on his return, built an exotic round church at Orphir, modelled on the Church of the Holy Sepulchre, Jerusalem.

The Orkneyinga Saga

Orkneyinga Saga, composed in Iceland in the early thirteenth century, gives a wealth of information about the tangled politics of the twelfth-century earldom. This is how we know so much about the murder of St Magnus, for instance. To its author, this was relatively recent history and so is probably reasonably accurate – although it was important to tell a good story, and wise not to be too rude about the Norwegian king's friends and relations. The saga is still a delight to read, insightful, funny and enthralling by turns.

Orkneyinga Saga also tells the story of Svein Asleifsson, a wealthy twelfth-century Orkney farmer and adventurer, whose lifestyle would not have been out of place several centuries earlier:

> This is how Svein used to live. Winter he would spend at home on Gairsay, where he entertained some 80 men at his own expense. His drinking hall was so big, there was nothing in Orkney to compare with it. In the spring he had more than enough to occupy him, with a great deal of seed to sow, which he saw to carefully himself. Then when that job was done, he would go off plundering in the Hebrides, and in Ireland on what he called his 'spring-trip', then back home just after midsummer, where he stayed till the cornfields had been reaped and the grain was safely in. After that he would go off raiding again, and never came back till the first month of winter was ended. This he used to call his 'winter-trip'.

Gairsay

Gairsay – the island home of Svein Asleifsson, a successful twelfth-century Norse rogue who, though fickle in his loyalties, always moved in high circles.
RICHARD WELSBY, STROMNESS

The Runic Alphabet

The Vikings were not illiterate and used runes to write magical formulae, inscriptions, graffiti or everyday messages on stone, bone, metal and wooden objects. Around 50 survive in Scotland.

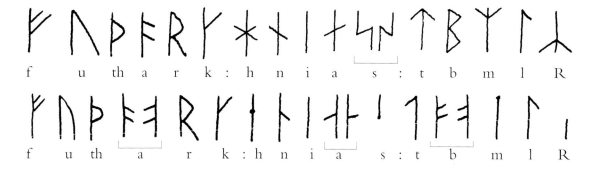

Maes Howe: a tomb rediscovered

One fascinating episode in the story of Scotland's Vikings occurred in 1153 when Norsemen broke into Maes Howe, a Neolithic chambered tomb on Orkney Mainland, and left a wealth of runic inscriptions all over its walls.

Some are simple graffiti of the 'Kilroy was here' variety: 'Ottarfila carved these runes.' Some are rude and funny: 'Ingibiorg the fair widow; many a woman has walked stooping in here; a very showy person', commenting on the view as an attractive woman made her way along the low entrance passage into the tomb; another is more respectful and romantic: 'Ingigerth is the most beautiful of women.' Then there was the braggart: 'These runes were carved by the man most skilled in runes in the western ocean ... with this axe owned by Gauk Trandilsson in the South Land' (i.e. southern Iceland).

Through the inscriptions we can almost speak to the invaders of Maes Howe. The runes tell us that: 'Crusaders broke into Maes Howe.' Why did they break into the mound? 'It is said to me that treasure is here hidden very well.' Who were these people? 'He is a Viking ... come here under this barrow.' So they could still call themselves Vikings. Were they a troop of renegades? 'Lif the earl's cook carved these runes'; the earl was the great Rognvald, who founded St Magnus Cathedral in Kirkwall.

Selection of Maes Howe Runes
One of many runic inscriptions carved in Maes Howe. The top line is written in cryptic twig-runes, while the others are standard runes. The inscription says: 'The man who is most skilled in runes west of the ocean carved these runes with the axe which Gaukr Trandilsson owned in the south of the country (Iceland).'
HISTORIC SCOTLAND

Maes Howe Interior when Opened in 1861
After the Vikings, Maes Howe was next broken into in 1861 by Mr Farrer, a prodigious digger of mounds, who has bequeathed us a set of wonderful drawings of how it looked then. (Inset: Maes Howe chambered tomb)
HISTORIC SCOTLAND

Carvings of Dragon and Knotted Serpent
The Norsemen did not only leave us messages in Maes Howe. They also carved the magnificent Maes Howe dragon – a direct descendant of Viking animal art – a knotted serpent and a slightly strange seal.
HISTORIC SCOTLAND

Cubbie Roo's Castle, Wyre
Kolbein Hruga's Castle, Wyre. This square stone tower stood
perhaps three storeys high originally, and was surrounded by a
defensive wall and outer ditch and bank.
HISTORIC SCOTLAND

Norse strongholds

It is extraordinary to think that, in the ninth
century, Norse overlords in the Northern Isles
were so confident of their control that they
had no need of strongholds. But by the twelfth
century, defensive sites were being built in the
earldom. 'At that time there lived [in Wyre] a
Norwegian called Kolbein Hruga, and he was
the most outstanding of men. He had a fine
stone castle built there; it was a safe strong-
hold', says the saga of events around 1150.
'Cubbie Roo's' Castle is thought to be the
earliest stone-built castle in Scotland. This
square stone tower, with 2m-thick mortared
walls, stood perhaps three storeys high originally, and was surrounded by another defensive
wall and outer ditch and bank. The Castle of
Old Wick, Caithness, was a similar twelfth-
century stone keep, perhaps built by Earl
Harald Maddadson.

The Norse were quite happy to use the
buildings of their predecessors when the need
arose. In 1153, Erland abducted Earl Harald's
mother and took refuge in the Iron Age Broch
of Mousa – 'an unhandy place to get at', says
the saga of this near-impregnable tower. This
wasn't the first time Mousa had proved useful:
around 900, an eloping couple took refuge
there after their ship was wrecked en route
from Norway to Iceland.

Castle of Strom, Shetland
Other early stone-built castles are hard to date accurately, but
several are probably Late Norse, such as this picturesque ruin on
an island in the Loch of Strom, Shetland Mainland.
HISTORIC SCOTLAND

Epilogue: the Viking Legacy

The end of the Viking Age ushered in a new social order and (with a few dishonourable exceptions like Svein Asleifsson) brought about the demise of the freebooting Viking chieftain. But the Vikings impressed their identity on different parts of the British Isles in many ways, and their legacy is still with us today.

The place-names of northern and western Scotland are a permanent testimonial to the thousands of men and women who travelled the sea road and made Scotland their home. Shetland and Orkney remained Scandinavian in language and customs for centuries after the Viking Age. The Norn language, descended from Old Norse, was still being spoken in the eighteenth century; and is evident in Shetland dialect today. Traditional implements of the Shetland crofthouse, farm and boat are hard to distinguish from their Norwegian counterparts – as are often their local names.

Trading links established between Scandinavia and the Northern Isles in the Viking Age persisted long afterwards, especially in Norway's timber for Orkney's grain; the old Custom House in Kirkwall is now the Norwegian Consulate, maintaining an age-old link. The Norse ancestry of the Ness yole, a traditional Shetland small boat, is apparent in its every line. The same type of Norse horizontal mill as discovered at Orphir continued in use into the present century in the islands; a well-preserved example survives at Click Mill, near Dounby, Orkney.

Examples of the Viking legacy abound in Orkney and Shetland, and today's visitor is immediately aware that the cultural heritage of these islands is different from that of the rest of Scotland. As for Orcadians and Shetlanders, they celebrate their Scandinavian inheritance in small and large ways day by day – in song and verse, customs and traditions, festivals and cultural links, and in continuing close relations with Norway and the other Scandinavian countries.

For those further away from the Scandinavian heartlands in Scotland, the reminders may only be echoes. But sometimes, in the city late at night, as the shipping forecast intones its hymn, the Viking sea road westwards is conjured from the shadows:

North Utsira – South Utsira (south-west Norway) – Viking – Cromarty – Forth – Irish Sea – Shannon – Rockall – Hebrides – Fair Isle – Faroes – south-east Iceland – expected soon.

Shetland Yole and Gokstad Rowing Boat
A twentieth-century Shetlandic Ness yole and the Viking rowing boat found in the Gokstad ship burial, Norway. The Norse ancestry of the yole is obvious.
SHETLAND MUSEUM
UNIVERSITETETS OLDSAKSAMLINGEN MED VIKINGSKIPSHUSET, OSLO, NORWAY

Sites Around Scotland

Sites to visit

Some of the best preserved settlements anywhere in the Viking world survive in Scotland, particularly in the Northern Isles; the list below is only a selection. A quick glance at the Ordnance Survey maps of the Northern or Western Isles will give a flavour of the many thousands of Scandinavian place-names still in use today, and it is mainly in these same areas that visible traces of Viking Age sites are especially evident.

The list follows the route of the Viking voyage in this book, progressing through the Orkney earldom, the Viking west, and lowland Scotland, with the sites listed by council area. The list focuses on monuments open to the public by Historic Scotland (marked HS) and by other bodies (marked P). Where there are no initials the site is on private land and the permission of the owner will be required. Ordnance Survey grid references are provided.

Shetland Islands

Jarlshof (HS) This well-preserved multi-period site is perhaps best known for its extensive Viking Age settlement, comprising an impressive complex of superimposed levels of longhouses and their outbuildings. There is also a small exhibition. HU 399 096.

Viking Unst The island of Unst is particularly rich in Viking Age remains. Norse longhouses are visible at several locations, including Hamar (HP 646 094), Underhoull (HP 573 044), and Sandwick (HP 618 023). The Norwegian king, Harald Finehair, anchored his fleet in the Unst bay which bears his name, Haraldswick.

Cunningsburgh The steatite quarries cover a large area on either side of the Catpund Burn. Traces of quarrying can be seen in the bed of the burn and on exposed rock outcrops to either side, above the road.

Most obvious are the projecting blanks for vessels that were never removed, round and rectangular depressions where blanks were removed, and chisel marks covering the rock faces. HU 426 272.

Law Ting Holm, Tingwall The open-air site of Shetland's first parliament juts into an inland loch in central Shetland. There are traces of a causeway and the circular stone enclosure where the *thing* actually met. HU 417 435.

Orkney Islands

Brough of Birsay (HS) On a beautiful tidal island off the NW corner of Orkney mainland are the remains of many Viking hall-houses and barns, together with a Norse blacksmith's workshop and a once grand entrance way or boat slipway, all adjacent to a fine twelfth-century church. The Norse buildings overlie a native Pictish settlement; a Pictish stone stands in the churchyard. HY 239 285.

Maes Howe (HS) Viking runic inscriptions and graffiti decorate the walls inside this magnificent 5000 year old chambered tomb. HY 363 127.

Orphir round church and Saga Centre (HS and P) An early twelfth-century round church, possibly built by Earl Hakon Paulsson, lies adjacent to the excavated remains of the earl's residence and a Norse water-mill. A visitor centre provides information on Norse sites mentioned in *Orkneyinga Saga*, including Orphir. HY 334 044.

St Magnus Cathdral and Bishop's Palace, Kirkwall (P) The building of the superb St Magnus Cathedral (still in use) was begun in 1137 by Earl Rognvald Kali Kolsson. The Bishop's Palace next door was built soon afterwards, when Kirkwall became the seat of the new Orkney bishopric. HY 449 108.

Brough of Deerness, Mainland (P) At this most dramatic spot, on a detached

promontory, is a Norse settlement of oblong buildings and a small stone chapel. HY 596 087.

Westness, Rousay The excavated Pictish and Viking cemetery lay on a low promontory with the remains of a boat noost and Viking Age farm nearby. Further west lie the remains of the 'Wirk', a probably twelfth-century Norse hall and tower. These all form part of the signposted Westness Walk, which also passes some magnificent prehistoric monuments and must be one of the richest archaeological miles in Britain. HY 375 293.

Pool, Sanday The island of Sanday is exceptionally rich in sites of all periods, many of them eroding out of the cliffs. Several millennia worth of the archaeological layers that make up the partly excavated farm mound at Pool can be seen in section from the beach, standing more than 3m high. HY 619 378.

St Boniface, Papa Westray (P) A walk along the beach here reveals extensive Iron Age, early Christian, Norse and medieval remains eroding out of the cliff. St Boniface's church, itself originally twelfth century in date, has recently been re-roofed and refurbished. HY 487 527.

St Magnus church, Egilsay (HS) The beautiful church of St Magnus, with its tall round tower, dominates the small island of Egilsay. Magnus was murdered here in 1117 at the order of his rival for the earldom, Earl Hakon. HY 466 303.

Cubbie Roo's Castle, Wyre (HS) The remains of this rare Norse castle, built by Kolbein Hruga in about 1150, stand close both to a twelfth-century church and a modern farm called Bu of Wyre. This farm name tells us that a great Norse hall preceded it and confirms that Wyre was the seat of a powerful Norse family. HY 441 263.

Tuquoy, Westray (partly HS) This important Viking, Late Norse and medieval settlement was the seat of a high status Norse family, which was responsible for the building of a fine twelfth-century church immediately adjacent. The remains of impressive stone buildings can be seen falling out of the cliff as you walk west along the beach from the church-yard. HY 455 431.

Highland
Freswick and Robertshaven An extensive Late Norse settlement among the sand dunes on Freswick Links overlies prehistoric remains. The rich Norse midden deposits visible eroding from the cliff edge have produced vast quantities of fish bones: evidence for large-scale fish processing at the site. Similar middens have been found at Robertshaven, near John O'Groats. ND 378 676 and ND 389 736 respectively.

Castle of Old Wick This plain keep tower is a Norse fortification, perched on a dramatic cliff promontory and cut off from the landward approach by a ditch. It probably dates from the late twelfth or thirteenth century. ND 369 488.

Old St Peter's Kirk, Thurso (P) A re-used stone high up in the west face of the church's tower wall is decorated with a 70cm-long runic inscription of the tenth century, commemorating a Viking woman called Gunnhildr. ND 120 686.

Western Isles
Bornish and Kilphedir, South Uist Three settlement mounds at Bornish conceal an extensive and complex Norse settlement: about 20 Viking Age buildings covering an area of some 0.8 hectares. The Kilphedir settlement some 10km to the south has been completely excavated but there are plans to build a reconstructed Viking house. NF 729 302 and NF 729 198.

The Udal, North Uist At this rich and complex multi-period site on the machair, the Norse took over a native settlement, probably in the later ninth century, and

built a fortlet and a cluster of sub-rectangular houses and outbuildings. NF 825 783.

Cnip, Uig, Lewis Pagan Viking and native graves are regularly exposed in eroding sand cliffs in the machair. The famous Lewis chessmen were also found in this general area. NB 100 365.

Blackhouse, Arnol, Lewis (HS) A traditional Lewis thatched longhouse with byre, attached barn and stackyard, complete and furnished. The longhouse tradition stretches back to the Viking Age. NB 310 492.

Argyll and Bute
Iona (HS) The first recorded Viking attack in Scotland was against Iona in 795. This wealthy early Christian monastery was attacked again and again over the next few years. NM 286 245.

Little Dunagoil, Bute Late Norse longhouses nestle within the enclosing wall of an earlier fort. The discovery of masses of lignite chippings suggest that the people who lived here made their living by working in lignite. NS 086 533.

Rothesay Castle, Bute (HS) This unusual castle, with its great circular curtain wall, was twice taken by the Norwegians: in 1230 after a siege; and again briefly in 1263, by King Haakon shortly before his defeat at the Battle of Largs. A video in the visitor centre tells the story. NS 088 646.

North Ayrshire
Largs (P) The end of the Viking west at the Battle of Largs in 1263 is celebrated at *Vikingar*, an innovative visitor centre by the sea within the modern town of Largs. The exhibits include reconstructed Viking houses and a replica boat. NS 202 600.

City of Glasgow
Govan (P) Govan Old parish church houses a rich collection of early historic sculptured stones, including five Viking Age hogbacks. The curving boundary of

the graveyard is a tell-tale sign of its early Christian origins. NS 553 659.

Fife
Inchcolm Abbey (HS) A Viking Age hogback tombstone is on show in the visitor centre on Inchcolm Island in the Firth of Forth, the site of the best-preserved group of monastic buildings in Scotland.

Danes Dyke and Constantine's Cave Popular tradition has it that Danes Dyke earthwork, which originally enclosed the Fife Ness promontory, was erected by Viking invaders in the ninth century. It still stands some 2m high at its south-eastern end (NO 635 096–634 096). According to tradition, King Constantine was captured by Vikings and put to death in Constantine's Cave. NO 633 101.

Dumfries and Galloway
Whithorn (HS) Recent excavations in a field adjacent to Whithorn Priory revealed extensive Northumbrian, Norse, medieval and later remains. The discoveries are explained in the visitor centre at this important monastic site. NX 444 403.

Kilmorie cross-slab This fine upright cross-slab, decorated with Celtic and Viking ornament, now stands in the garden to the east of Corsewall House. NX 032 690.

Museums
Some of the archaeological sites listed above also have small exhibitions of finds (e.g. Brough of Birsay; Whithorn). Many of the finest Viking Age artefacts are housed in the new Museum of Scotland, Chambers Street, Edinburgh, including most of the Viking silver hoards and the finds from pagan Viking graves. Tankerness House Museum, in Kirkwall, Orkney, also houses a good collection of finds, notably those from the Scar boat burial; and some of the Viking Age finds from Shetland can be seen in Shetland County Museum, Lerwick. Some smaller museums also contain important collections of Viking Age artefacts, such as: Western Isles Museum, Stornoway, Lewis; Rothesay Museum, Bute; and Stranraer Museum, in Galloway.

Further Reading

Scandinavian Scotland, Barbara Crawford (Leicester University Press 1987).

Viking Scotland, Anna Ritchie (Historic Scotland/Batsford 1993).

Vikings in Scotland, an archaeological survey, James Graham-Campbell and Colleen Batey (Edinburgh University Press 1998).

The Viking Age in Caithness, Orkney and the North Atlantic, edited by Colleen Batey, Judith Jesch and Christopher Morris (Edinburgh University Press 1993) contains papers about many of the sites featured here.

Scandinavian settlement in Northern Britain, edited by Barbara Crawford (which focuses on place-name evidence) (Leicester University Press 1995).

The Viking-Age gold and silver of Scotland, James Graham-Campbell (National Museums of Scotland 1995).

Historic Scotland's guidebooks on relevant sites in state care (e.g. Jarlshof, Brough of Birsay, Maes Howe) are also very useful, as are its more general books, *Invaders of Scotland*, *The ancient monuments of Orkney*, *The ancient monuments of Shetland* and *The ancient monuments of the Western Isles*. For a good introduction to the parallel story in England, see: *Viking Age England*, Julian Richards (English Heritage/Batsford 1991).

FOR MORE GENERAL BOOKS ON THE VIKINGS, SEE:

Cultural Atlas of the Viking World, James Graham-Campbell (Andromeda Oxford Ltd 1994).

Follow the Vikings, edited by Dan Carlsson and Olwyn Owen (Viking Heritage, Gotland, for the Council of Europe 1996).

Oxford Illustrated History of the Vikings, Peter Sawyer (Oxford University Press 1997).

Acknowledgements

I am very grateful to the many friends and colleagues who have helped during preparation of this book, particularly Julie Gibson and Val Turner (Orkney and Shetland Island Archaeologists respectively), and all those archaeologists who provided pictures and information on their sites ahead of publication (named below). I am especially grateful to Gordon Barclay for his general encouragement and editorial assistance; Dr Barbara Crawford who kindly commented on an earlier draft; Matt Ritchie for help with picture research; David Simon for his excellent reconstruction drawings; and Rob Burns for preparing the maps.

Thanks are due to the following organisations and individuals for permission to reproduce their copyright illustrations: Historic Scotland (Crown Copyright); The Royal Commission on Ancient and Historical Monuments of Scotland (Crown Copyright); The Trustees of the National Museums of Scotland; Vikingeskibshallen I Roskilde, Denmark; Universitetets Oldsaksamlingen med Vikingskipshuset, Oslo, Norway; Bryggens Museum, Bergen, Norway; The Pierpoint Morgan Library, New York, USA; Musée Anne de Beaujeu, Moulins, France; The Orkney Library (Orkney Islands Council); Shetland Museum (Shetland Islands Council); College of Cardiff, University of Wales; University of Sheffield; Centre for Field Archaeology, University of Edinburgh; Scottish Urban Archaeological Trust; Rover Group Ltd; Dennis Coutts Photography; T. E. Gray Photography; Richard Welsby Photography; Professor Mick Aston (and Channel 4's *Time Team*); Magnar Dalland; Professor John Hunter; Headland Archaeology Ltd, The Whithorn Trust, Dr Raymond Lamb; Dr Christopher Lowe; David MacCullough; Professor Christopher Morris; Dr Mike Parker-Pearson; Niall Sharples; and Christina Unwin.

HISTORIC SCOTLAND safeguards Scotland's built heritage, including its archaeology, and promotes its understanding and enjoyment on behalf of the Secretary of State for Scotland. It undertakes a programme of 'rescue archaeology', from which many of the results are published in this book series.

Scotland has a wealth of ancient monuments and historic buildings, ranging from prehistoric tombs and settlements to remains from the Second World War, and HISTORIC SCOTLAND gives legal protection to the most important, guarding them against damaging changes or destruction. HISTORIC SCOTLAND gives grants and advice to the owners and occupiers of these sites and buildings.

HISTORIC SCOTLAND has membership scheme which allows access to properties in its care, as well as other benefits.
For information, contact:
0131 668 8999.